FREE BONUS!

As a valued reader, and to thank you for your purchase, we invite you to download a complimentary eBook: 36 Highly Effective Habits.

Scan the QR code below, subscribe to the **Origami Editions** newsletter, and access your free copy in less than 2 minutes.

You will also occasionally receive curated self-development tools, updates on upcoming releases, exclusive offers, and resources to support your personal and professional growth journey.

Reading for Better Living.

CONTENTS

EMOTIONAL INTELLIGENCE THEORY

EMOTIONAL INTELLIGENCE THEORY

Valentin Waldman

ORIGAMI EDITIONS
READING FOR BETTER LIVING

BETTER YOU SERIES

To you, Papy
—My forever inspiration.

Contents

INTRODUCTION

There's something called the 80:20 rule, and it keeps cropping up in life, business, and pretty much everywhere. It got a proper name, the Pareto Principle, after an Italian economist observed that 80% of an outcome comes from 20% of a specific cause. He stated that 80% of a country's wealth is held by 20% of its population. And since then, the same rule has been applied to productivity, sales, and relationships.

A concrete example could be that 80% of a company's sales results come from 20% of the efforts deployed to achieve those results. Consider this: It could encompass the time spent thinking strategically, meeting clients, and maintaining relationships with them while excluding lower-impact activities, such as developing marketing materials or keeping the database up to date.

Now, here's the connection to our subject—being efficient in emotional intelligence (often abbreviated as EI) can effectively and meaningfully lead and manage others, accounting for 80% of the outcome.

A typical manager in a typical business (if there are typical managers in typical businesses) will spend much of their time managing other people, from maximizing the skills of their employees to motivating them. That means the vast majority of their time is spent getting the best out of other people; their own skills got them to this position, but they are now compounding the effect by gaining a whole new range of skills to harness the expertise of each team member.

Take the floor manager of a busy department store. She has worked her way up through the ranks. Before her promotion, she was the top sales assistant of the year for three consecutive years; there's not much she doesn't know about making sales, and nobody doubts her core customer management skills. But she now has twenty-four people reporting to her, covering white goods, bedding, entertainment, and children's clothing.

She is ultimately responsible for their training, welfare, and advancement, as well as the sales and profit performance of the whole floor. She helps when a customer requests something while she is hurrying to a recruitment or promotions meeting, but she has to pass that keen customer on to one of her sales assistants.

Of course, every so often, a customer turns up when the sales floor manager has the time, which means she can delight in utilizing her hard-won direct selling skills that attracted her to retail in the first place. But the critical thing to take away is that this floor manager's responsibility is not selling anymore; it is to multiply her experience and expertise by encouraging the twenty-four people who work for her to be as enthusiastic as her, to love their job every bit as much as she does, and produce enough sales to fulfill the ambitious objectives. Getting people to perform at their best becomes her 20%, and she must be excellent at it to be successful.

This involves obvious aspects, such as people relationships, being inspiring, encouragement, motivation, and goal alignment, but also less obvious aspects, such as working to reduce barriers to sales across the entire department store floor. This multiplier of positivity is what the *Emotional Intelligence Theory* is about; the more you can spread meaningful emotions, resulting in a positive relationship dynamic, the more everyone benefits in the ultimate virtuous circle. This involves several principles, with emotional intelligence being the primary aspect positively impacting working relationships. These principles will be explained in the early chapters of this book. Essentially, it involves subscribing to emotional intelligence and leveraging it for everyone's benefit and growth.

With people management comes great responsibility, as it has the potential to make lasting impacts on others' lives. This book is precisely about getting the multiplier effect to ripple through your workplace; it's about gaining and using emotional intelligence to inspire others around you, including employees, but not only, to give their very best and for you to make the most of the 20% making up the 80% of your desired outcome.

Effective people management involves adhering to principles that involve sensitive leadership, effective communication, empathy, and motivating people to step out of their comfort zones and strive for the collective objective, whether maximizing sales or sending a person to Mars.

It's about leveraging what you have as a team and utilizing it to the best advantage through open and thoughtful management.

THE NEW REALITY OF DOING BUSINESS

Most people start work in their late teens or early twenties and continue through retirement, usually in their sixties, although some stop earlier and a lot go on much longer. Necessity and enjoyment come into the equation, so making general observations is challenging; everyone has a different perspective on what work involves. In the old days, most people left their homes and worked in offices, factories, or government agencies. That mold broke a few years ago. Most people date the change to the various COVID lockdowns, but that's not quite right. That was the spark, but the fire had been smoldering for a long time. The fuel was technology, slowly changing how we view work, reviewing our lifestyle, seeing more opportunity in the digital world, and how we lead the people behind computers.

A broad estimate is that over half the workforce is either Gen Z or Millennials, with a birth range from the early eighties until the early teens of the current century. That means these categories will increase as a proportion of the workforce over the next decade, with someone born in 2013 turning 22 in 2035.

'So what?' you might think. But there is a crucial concept to grasp here, as the two categories of people described have grown up with technology and know it inherently, absolutely, and intimately. For instance, they're fully comfortable with remote working, and you even get the concept of the digital nomad or the traveling entrepreneur. That means everything is changing around us, and the clever managers of today and tomorrow are adapting adroitly to take advantage of the situation.

I started with a department store as an example precisely because it is an industry that has seen dramatic changes. With more shopping done online than ever, and AI becoming increasingly present every day, it is unlikely to go backward anytime soon. This is the case in most industries, except for a few exceptions.

Something counterintuitive is that humans will always need human interactions and socialization. Retail is changing rapidly, and some department stores that have not kept up with the changes have gone out of business. All stores now have a significant online presence, so leaders must adapt to manage teams remotely.

But, because there is always a 'but,' things change constantly, such that many people observe that the only constant is change. Think back to how it might have been twenty or thirty years ago. If you wanted to make a purchase, you would get in your car on the weekend, fight for a parking spot at the nearest mall, and then wade through the crowds to get to the store you needed. Now, for many items, you open your laptop at any time of the week, make a few clicks, and then sit back and wait for your dog food, garden fork, new dress, or whatever to arrive. Behind your few clicks, there's still an army of people working away in new jobs, doing tasks that were never necessary before, with controls people a generation earlier hadn't dreamt up yet, but creating wealth in brand-new ways.

Now, I hear the point being made isn't that just changing one job for another? Yes, is the answer to that question, at least a lot of the time. But take the toll booth as an example. Few of these are now handled by human beings doing dreary, low-paid work, where they wish the time away. The new positions are in software development, digital activities, automated machinery design and manufacture, and marketing, with a focus on rolling out the sales of brand-new technology.

We are exchanging one job for another, but it is exchanging tedium and all the stress that comes with it for exciting new skill development that opens up new opportunities now and for the future.

That's the world of work that leaders are 'managing' today. And it's going to go a lot further down that particular track. There is one overriding aspect of this new world of work. People today expect to contribute to the success of the businesses they work in. They want to be included and consulted, and the clever manager will realize that two, five, ten, or more brains are an awful lot better than one.

Take a look at factories because they make the point perfectly. Forty or fifty years ago, a lot of the factories, wherever in the world, were rife with work-to-rule. When the bell went for the end of shift and the gates opened, the workers had been hanging around inside, just waiting for their freedom, thousands pouring out together to jam up the approach roads. Nowadays, that would be a perfect recipe for bankruptcy. Manual work has been replaced by machinery, and employees can contribute to more interesting activities (precisely because machines cannot replace them) while being a thousand kilometers away from colleagues and still able to socialize with them through calls and other technological means.

The factory has just gotten better.

Think about change as an exponential curve. Wherever you are on that curve, you face change. That's because the world is constantly changing, but that curve gets steeper as you go left to right. The pace of change is accelerating. The world is changing, as is the available technology (the main driver of that change), and the people coming into the workforce are different, too. What worked well for your grandparents would never work well today.

In Japanese society post WWII, companies notoriously hired for life. Stability and permanence were twin pillars of the world of work. Overall, the Japanese industry performed surprisingly well, coming to dominate key product areas such as cars, motorcycles, machinery, and others. The culture at their workplaces stressed loyalty; it was not unusual for a graduate to stay with the same employer from their first day to the last, the day of their retirement.

But everything moves on.

A generation ago, it was considered job-hopping (a bad thing) if your resume showed you had spent less than 3-5 years on the same job. Nowadays, the younger generation are often freelancers or simultaneously hold several part-time jobs. It's turned on a dime so that the old idea of loyalty and longevity can be seen as a lack of experience, or even timidity. Loyalty was expected from old-school employers—demanded, even. Nowadays, firms must earn that loyalty through an open and inclusive approach to management, though, as we shall see, the emotional theory fits perfectly.

Two key things underpin this new approach to work. The first is technology, and the second is work-life balance.

Technology can be confusing, frustrating, and threatening, especially if your resume states you've been a hermit for the last two decades. But, more often than not, it can be liberating and, taken properly, that's enough to outweigh all the negatives.

What does this mean? It means there's been a divorce between employees and the workplace. The millstone everyone wore around their necks (typically associated with offices, warehouses, or factories) has been cut loose by the sharp blade of technology. People can, with certain limitations, work and live in different places altogether.

And the modern leader must find a way through this, thereby gaining the full range of benefits available through staff motivation and creating a shared purpose.

What does that mean in practice?

It comes down to the enlightenment of modern leaders, who have abandoned their authoritarian approach and have found open and meaningful ways to lead, making work an extension of life and as much fun as anything else.

This is where the work-life balance comes in, doubling the potential gain but probably trebling the risk of getting it all wrong. Gen Z and Millennials, in particular, have entered the workforce with an exceptional sense of work-life balance. Like the old joke about the French living to eat, whereas other countries eat to live, the older generations could be accused of living to work.

Well, that's all changed; the latest two generations hitting the working world have an infinitely better perspective on this, altering the established priorities entirely.

That means leaders attuned to these powerful trends will do much better at getting the best from their staff than those who daydream about how it used to be.

In most instances, how it used to be doesn't work at work anymore. Instead, there is a need for flexibility, open communication, and a significant dose of understanding, which we refer to as emotional intelligence, as this book will illustrate.

The concept of working for someone has undergone a radical transformation. Back in the 'old days,' one followed the instructions of one's boss almost blindly; certainly, questioning his or her decisions would be frowned upon. 'The boss' was a cardboard figure who issued orders and expected everyone to toe the line.

Now, people want to work for someone who invests everything in the business in a thoughtful and enlightened manner. Work-life balance isn't so much about reducing your hours; it's about fusing the two into life. To achieve this, each individual needs to feel fulfilled and believe that their contribution is valued.

This aligns neatly with the *Emotional Intelligence Theory* that this book expounds upon.

THE EMOTIONAL INTELLIGENCE REVOLUTION

We are discussing a new style of management that overturns traditional hierarchies. It's a holistic approach, one that is far better than that hole in the sand that's presenting itself as the alternative. This book refers to this new management approach as the *Emotional Intelligence Theory*, with each of those words carrying significant meaning.

Emotional Intelligence is the ability to become self-aware, to know yourself and connect with others by seeing life from their point of view, or putting yourself in someone else's shoes, and adapting your expression of emotions in a way that leads to positive impacts. Remember how vital this is for the Gen Z and Millennial generations, who rightfully want to be understood and have so much to offer to those who will meet them, even halfway.

Theory means that the proposed method of applying emotional intelligence is a proven, efficient, well-developed set of ideas. You can get ahead by following these practices; it will give you the edge, the advantage you need to excel with your team and in life in general, because, thankfully, emotional intelligence does extend beyond your professional environment, becoming a built-in quality. It creates something far more powerful than regular management, where your team does things you ask them to, specifically because it's tailored and personalized to fit each person's personality, purposely bringing out the best of what they can offer.

In other words, it is your way to get the best outcome of people's interactions, a concept we will investigate thoroughly throughout this book.

In the definition of emotional intelligence provided earlier, did you notice that self-awareness was the beginning of the self-formulated definition? This was purposely the case because if emotional intelligence is a cocktail of abilities, it starts with self-awareness—in other words, knowing yourself, in particular, how you react to certain situations and how your attitude and emotions impact your actions.

There are thousands of books spanning centuries on understanding the inner self. The Ancient Greeks had a lot to say about this, and the vital quality running through every single book on the subject is honesty. If you act in a manner that is out of line with who you are, you're being dishonest. And the perpetrator and the victim of that dishonesty are the same person because you're committing fraud upon yourself.

How many times have you heard a comment like, 'I just don't trust him'? Trust is a fundamental quality in any human relationship. That does not mean all relationships must have it: People, governments, companies, and countries all have relationships where trust is absent. However, it becomes a vital component to get the most out of every situation involving people interaction.

Take that back a stage further, building trust requires openness and honesty. Strangely, saying, 'I don't like how you handled that matter,' actually can build trust because of the honesty implied. If you had heaped praise instead while secretly detesting the way they had gone about it, that would come out some time later, destroying any trust that had been built up beforehand.

Trust is a crucial aspect of modern management and leadership.

So, the first building block of our new emotional intelligence mansion is self-awareness, but before we lay that stone, we need to pour honesty into the foundations. Next comes a little control, because, sadly, knowing your own emotions and responses to events and people is only the first step.

You need to practice self-regulation, which involves controlling or regulating your emotions. From that point, it's a relatively straightforward step toward developing empathy, which is another key to unlocking emotional intelligence. Remember, empathy is the ability to put yourself in other people's shoes, to see things from their perspective. Once you know yourself and can control your emotions, you're in a far better place to set goals and take others along with you because, with your newfound empathy, you can picture what it's like for them, too. Through empathy, you build a relationship of understanding and trust, which is a massive benefit in long-term relationships.

This book will also develop two other vital components of emotional intelligence: psychological intelligence and emotional agility.

Psychological intelligence and emotional agility are ways to understand others (their responses, reactions, and feelings to any situation or development of events) and to have the skillset to react appropriately. In other words, it involves having the maturity of emotions to know how to adapt and respond positively to someone, thus getting the best out of them in a wide variety of different circumstances.

Add a dose of effective communication and basic management skills, and you're there. You have become an emotionally intelligent person, which is the mission of this book.

People with emotional intelligence can unlock situations, negotiate effectively, and get to the heart and soul of the human beings they interact with.

You will see from the building blocks that we are discussing the importance of connecting with others, utilizing awareness of their emotions, and motivation to build bridges of communication. The *Emotional Intelligence Theory* is diametrically opposed to Hierarchical Alienation, the concept that many businesses were built upon in the past and that some corporations still seem to adhere to. It brings together all the skills and abilities of every member of the team in an inclusive cooperation that harnesses all that power and focuses it on a common cause. It means everyone is driving forward toward the same goal, the same objective. This has a multiplying effect because the individual employee feels valued and respected, which motivates them to contribute further to the business's development, often in an exponential manner and truly from their heart. There are few to no internal factions and infighting in a team managed this way. Employees are no longer looking at each other as competitors, but rather as teammates working toward the same goals, because they are listened to and respected and have been taught to collaborate, hand in hand.

Squabbling in the workplace often stems from uncertainty, typically caused by poor communication, overpowering attitudes, and office politics.

Yet, we know that such a method no longer works with the generations we are trying to appeal to. In the past, other people may have performed tasks because they were instructed to do so. They may have done it well, but they probably did not put their heart and soul into it for the simple reason that their heart and soul were somewhere else. They might have been with their families, on sports fields, on a dream vacation, or worrying endlessly about rumors of redundancies. Wherever their minds were, they were only minimally focused on the company's mission.

Emotional Intelligence, as explored within the theory, is holistic in temperament. It wants to look after the whole person so that the entire person can give back. The 'whole person' concept is integral to this philosophy in another key way, as the empathetic approach to management cannot be applied sporadically. It is a whole-time method, one that must be practiced consistently to achieve maximum benefits. It is an attitude that prevails, rather than one that can be adopted for an individual task and then set aside.

Imagine the type of work environment you're creating if one minute you, as the leader, turn from being very receptive and inspiring with your team, only to fall back at a later stage to some old, authoritarian, and outdated management style. It's a reasonable bet that this will cause a significant setback because the people reporting to you will never know which line you are going to take, with insecurity and distrust taking over any positive emotions you were trying to build.

Consistency is absolutely key. This involves developing a meaningful and effective attitude, rather than dipping in and out of it from time to time.

A distinct bonus comes from the fact that the more you apply yourself to the *Emotional Intelligence Theory*, the better you will become at it. The *Emotional Intelligence Theory* becomes easier to achieve over time.

It also becomes easier because the more you practice with consistency, the more your team members enjoy interacting with you, and this enjoyment spreads from manager to supervisor and from supervisor to individual contributors.

Like any learning program, starting with the building blocks is essential, and the *Emotional Intelligence Theory* is no exception. I invite you to thoroughly explore the necessary foundations of this theory, including the concept of emotional intelligence and adaptability, through this book, knowing that this will enable you to lead others toward success.

As the ancient Chinese philosopher Laozi (circa 6th century BCE) said, *"A journey of a thousand miles begins with a single step."*

PART 1
EMOTIONAL
INTELLIGENCE THEORY

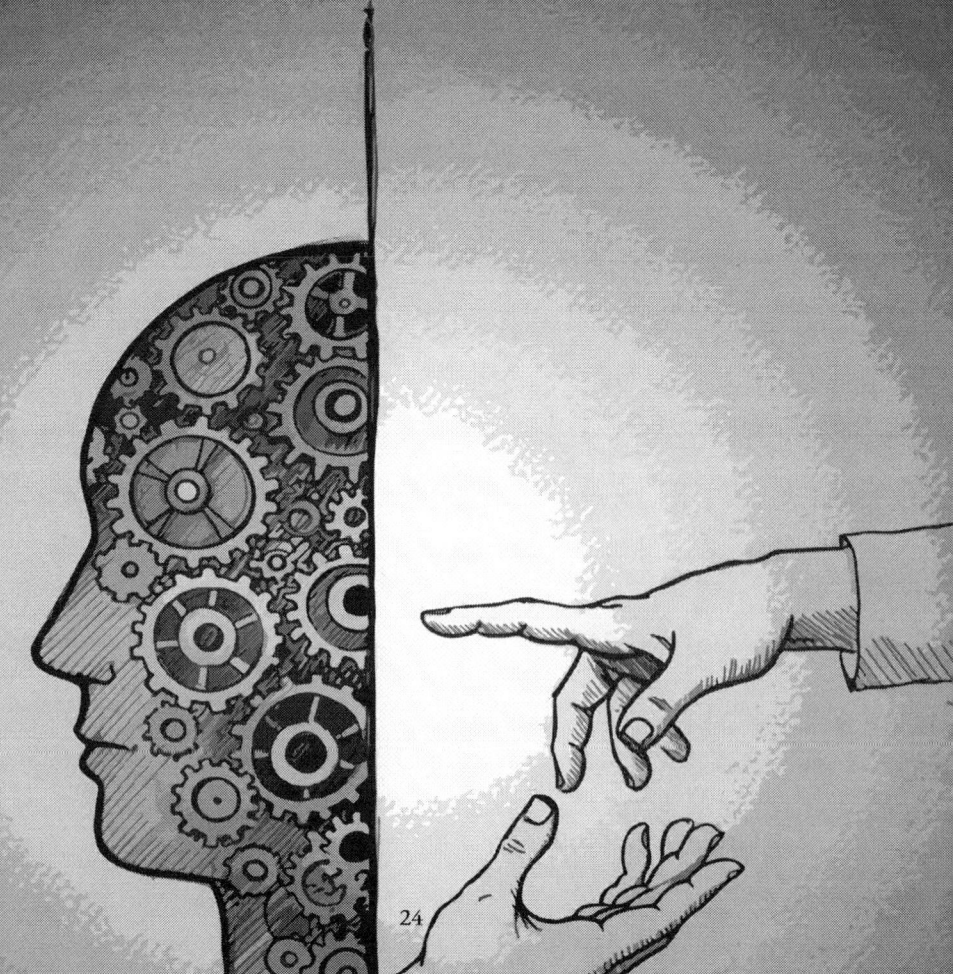

CHAPTER

1

WHAT IS THE EMOTIONAL INTELLIGENCE THEORY?

> *"Seeing with the eyes of another, listening with the ears of another, and feeling with the heart of another."*
> *— Alfred Adler, Austrian psychiatrist*

Alfred Adler (1870-1937) was an Austrian psychiatrist best known for introducing the concept of the "inferiority complex," which stemmed from his early focus on this concept. However, he made an equally long-lasting contribution to thinking about empathy. He emphasized the individual in terms of psychology (that is, a person as a whole), founding his school of thought, which he called the School of Individual Psychology. Thus, in his way, Alfred Adler was a pioneer of the emergence of the concept of emotional intelligence.

So, what is the *Emotional Intelligence Theory*? Quite simply, it involves the application of emotional intelligence based on a set of principles outlined in this chapter, with its use further explained throughout this book.

In other words, the ability to 'see with the eyes of another,' combined with the determination to 'walk a mile' in someone else's shoes.

And the beauty of it, apart from the fact it promotes understanding, compromise, and cooperation, as if that isn't enough?

The beauty is that it's not a talent you either possess or don't; it's a set of principles that can be learned by just about everyone.

Of course, there are exceptions. Adolf Hitler, for example, is generally thought to be a psychopath, a symptom of which is a severe lack of empathy. Thankfully, Hitler is an exception to the rule that most people can develop empathy through practice, study, and self-reflection—empathy that then spreads in a virtuous circle, inspiring more of itself.

THE EMOTIONAL INTELLIGENCE THEORY PRINCIPLES

We're overdue in describing the principles on which the *Emotional Intelligence Theory* is based:

First Principle: The Leading Principle

Leading with emotional intelligence, prioritizing empathetic decisions, and adopting a compassionate management style yields long-term benefits that outweigh short-term disadvantages.

For this reason, the empathetic management style, which we will learn to practice, becomes the default management style.

Picture the office when a deadline is looming, and it means all hands on deck as the follow-up contract depends on the successful conclusion of this prototype version. One approach might be to block everyone from going outside until you're satisfied the work is complete. But you've got mothers working with you who have young kids to care for, your assistant manager's father is at the hospital, and you know your PA is itching to see the school play in which her daughter has the lead role in. Somehow, because you can see their points of view, you know instinctively that the 'all-hands-on-deck' approach isn't right. You gather everyone around, dragging the copywriter out from under his desk, and explain the situation. You may get one or two questions, often from those who have not yet mastered emotional intelligence, but generally speaking, you get a bounce in morale that steers you through. You make the deadline after an all-nighter with five minutes to spare. You might have been able to do it another way, but you've built something positive and lasting because you've exercised your emotional intelligence and built a team around it. You have made empathetic decisions and led by example, showing others how to lead in the future.

Yet, you could wonder where the long-term benefit of this example is. That leads us nicely to the following principles.

Second Principle: The Butterfly Effect

Employees essentially look up to their managers and mirror their behavior. Therefore, when a manager is empathetic, it invites employees to apply the same empathy, which in turn benefits customers, the company, and the people they work with.

It's an old cliché that the business is nothing without people. But most old clichés are around for a reason—they happen to be true. Now, step back a moment and look at that cliché again. What does it mean? Well, people are the business in two distinct ways: First, they interact with your clients, probably even more than you in some cases. Second, they work together, bringing a range of skills and expertise. Now ask yourself: Do you want empathetic employees to interact with your customers, their colleagues, and yourself, or emotionally insensitive people? Now think: Who do you think should set this inspiring example?

It all starts with you, and to illustrate it, we're going to bring in another old cliché: imitation is the sincerest form of flattery. Whether Oscar Wilde originated this saying or it predates him does not matter. What matters is that the spreading effect of emotional intelligence, empathy, and compassion is evident as people see it working, and try it out for themselves.

Third Principle: The Virtuous Circle

Employees are consciously or unconsciously aligning themselves for the benefit or detriment of their managers, and for this reason, managers should apply empathy and care to benefit from positive attraction.

Emotional intelligence is your ability to recognize, understand, and manage both your own emotions and those of others. Yes, you ran right up against the deadline, but it doesn't stop there. Inevitably, by the next deadline, you will have a bank of loyalty and appreciation to fuel your next effort. Not only that, but your PA also told several people around her, both within and outside your organization, such as her daughter's school, about how good it feels to work for someone with an inspiring level of understanding. Word spreads, and not only is the team spirit healthy, but next time you're advertising a vacancy, you get floods of high-quality applicants and can build out the depth of your department even more. You have created something from nothing but an empathetic attitude, something that will benefit the organization for a long time to come. But let's move on because that is how much of a business's success derives.

We are all judges of the people who lead. It's human nature to compare how one person manages their department with another. We create a league table and develop favorites we want to work for and those for whom we would never. People are human, meaning the better you treat them, the more they're going to sing your praises when it comes to gossip by the coffee machine. That is going to make others wish they were in sales instead of marketing, or vice versa. They want to follow someone they appreciate and who inspires them, and the effort they make when they get the chance is definitely a form of payback for the empathy you've shown.

Fourth Principle: Understanding Others and Adapting Your Emotions

Using emotional agility to deal with others is essential in people management; therefore, a manager must develop psychological intelligence to read personalities and emotions effectively, to best respond to them.

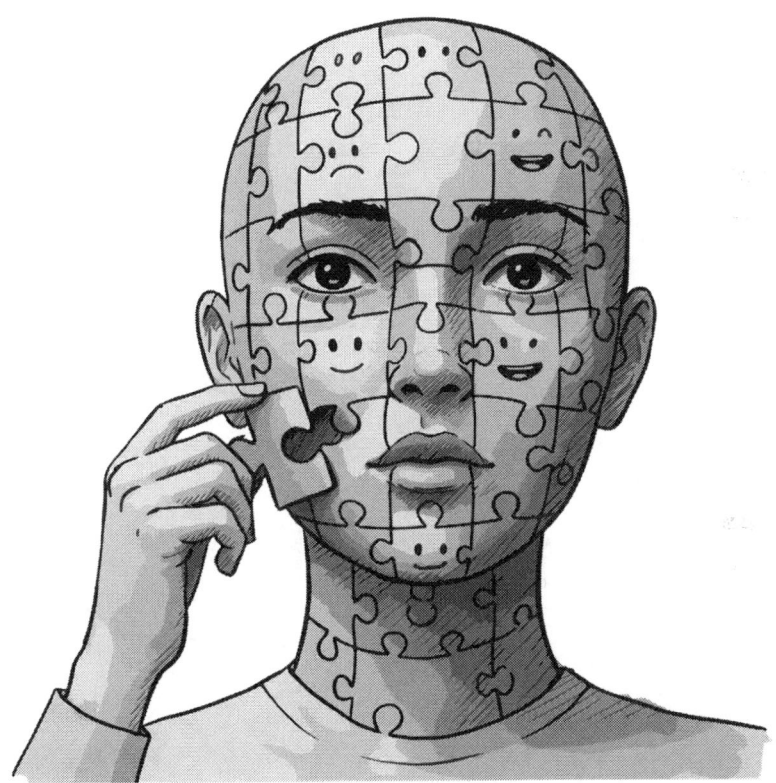

    This principle is double-barreled because it has two arms: psychological intelligence, which is your ability to understand how people react and behave in particular circumstances, and emotional agility, which is your capacity to adapt your emotions to best respond to others' emotions. In other words, you need to understand others and manage your emotions to interact most effectively with them.

Fifth Principle: Be Authentic

Being yourself is essential to interact with others meaningfully, and authenticity can only be comfortably lived in the right environment. If it is lived in the right environment, it unavoidably leads to success.

To your pleasure, we will continue with the third of our trio of clichés, the saying, 'Just be yourself.' It's generally held that people who are true to themselves find more long-term success and happiness than those who 'perform' to what they conceive to be expected of them. Hence, authenticity—being true to who you really are—is a vital component of applying emotional intelligence, empathy, and compassion, which we all strive for. You cannot deceive others, at least, not in the long term.

THE EMOTIONAL INTELLIGENCE THEORY BENEFITS

The principles behind the *Emotional Intelligence Theory* are varied, fundamental, and well worth mastering because they give your people management an edge compared to other traditional management methods. 'Mastering' is an interesting choice of word, generally referring to obtaining specific skill sets. However, with the *Emotional Intelligence Theory,* we're talking about the ability to master an attitude; you change your approach and realize the benefits, as it becomes a natural position to take.

In other words, you operate at a deeper level in which the skills of listening, understanding, and interacting are controlled by the set of principles you have developed.

Fundamental to the *Emotional Intelligence Theory* is the concept of building and caring relationships, allowing the benefits to ripple outward and create more advantages over time. It's the accumulation of these benefits that makes the value to any business. Just as *more hands make light work* and *two heads are better than one*, it stands to reason that if you can harness the genuine passion and skills coming from the heart of individuals working in your department, you add to your joint capabilities considerably.

Another key facet of this approach is the knock-on effect they produce, whereby the initial achievement keeps growing and growing, attracting sympathy and dedication, creating a positive work environment, and attracting the best talents. You can end up with a well-run ship, where the crew knows exactly what to do and has a fierce determination to work as a team to push their mission forward because they know who and what they are working for and appreciate it.

In other words, it cements your leadership.

Let's take an example:

Frank earned his position as sales manager by bringing in record business and developing several key customers who had remained outside their customer circle for too long. He knew himself well, having reflected on his strengths and weaknesses as he rose further at Design Inc., a rapidly growing startup, that while he could bring the business in, he was not the type to organize the delivery of the design projects. At first, he struggled with this, but a chat with the VP of Sales led him to a solution. To cut a long story short, he recruited a new assistant, Jacqui, with a plan that he would bring in the orders and she would deliver them. She, being a great organizer.

As more business came in and the quality of delivery improved, Frank's department grew in size. Due to his renowned thoughtfulness and caring approach to those working for him, which builds on their existing skills and provides opportunities for development and growth, he attracted a flood of people wanting to work for him, following the mantra that *success breeds success*. That brought new talent and new ideas into the mix, and one day Frank took the plunge. He and Jacquie presented an idea to bring in business from a new and untapped source market to the board.

The directors considered this and moved forward, citing the positive can-do attitude they had developed in their department.

Essentially, Frank no longer saw it as his department but as theirs— free of unwanted ego and rich in thinking *people first*.

FIRST PRINCIPLE
THE LEADING PRINCIPLE

Leading with emotional intelligence, prioritizing empathetic decisions, and adopting a compassionate management style yields long-term benefits that outweigh short-term disadvantages.

CHAPTER

EMOTIONAL INTELLIGENCE: CONNECTING THEORY AND PRACTICE

"Empathy is the greatest virtue. From it, all other virtues flow. Without it, all virtues are an act."
— Eric Zorn, U.S. columnist and writer

DEFINITION

Always start with a definition and take it from there. We discussed emotional intelligence in the previous chapter, which involves understanding and connecting with emotions, enabling the emotionally intelligent person to manage those emotions, thereby stimulating the best outcomes around that person. Let's go for an academic definition:

> *Emotional intelligence is the ability to recognize, understand, and manage both your own emotions and those of others.*[1]

You will find other definitions, but they essentially all mean the same thing, and I like this one for its compartmental nature and its simplicity.

Now, let's break this definition down by part:

Recognition: Noticing the existence of emotion (it could be anything from fear to hope and back again), and an awareness of its importance.

Understanding: Appreciating the significance of the recognized emotion, which necessitates knowing in broad terms what it is—envy, ambition, satisfaction, courage, loyalty, and so on. One should make a mental note here that not all emotions fit into precise buckets. Hence, it might be that you encounter satisfaction with a degree of loyalty attached, or ambition mixed with envy. The important thing here is that you have your antennae up in receiving mode; to a certain extent, you can trust your instinct, especially as you get more experienced in interpreting emotions, which, at first, might seem to be a sea washing all over you. But you will get there. Remember, emotional intelligence is something you can learn and then practice, improving with each passing day.

Managing involves recognizing and understanding the stated stages, combining them with your experience and some knowledge of what you're trying to achieve. Whether it's your own emotions or those of others, it's the same approach to ensure you, or they, react in the best possible way to the situation you find yourselves in.

---

[1] *Daniel Goleman: Emotional Intelligence: Why It Can Matter More Than IQ (1995).*

Essentially, emotional intelligence is about understanding and connecting with emotions and being aware of how they may impact any given situation, whether you are dealing with your own emotions or the emotions of people you interact with. It's the awareness of emotion that we will take into the next stage of our journey.

FROM EMOTIONAL INTELLIGENCE THEORY TO ITS PRACTICE

Any look at the connection between these two must rest on an understanding of what they are. We know from the previous section that emotional intelligence is, in general terms, an appreciation and awareness of emotions, whether those emotions sit inside you or someone else. It is practiced utilizing this awareness and these skills to your or your group's advantage.

From Chapter 1, we understand what the *Emotional Intelligence Theory* is, namely, the principles from which understanding and practicing empathy, as well as a generally emotionally intelligent attitude, derive their meaning.

So, we have two closely associated concepts. The *Emotional Intelligence Theory* is a set of principles and a framework that guides individuals in practicing emotional intelligence, encompassing empathy, compassion, and other key concepts. Emotional intelligence lies somewhere between a state of mind and a skill set; it is the driving force behind your interactions with people.

Let's recap on what we have discussed in the most concise way possible, based on the quotation from Daniel Goleman, that *emotional intelligence is the ability to recognize, understand, and manage both your own emotions and those of others:*

- The *Emotional Intelligence Theory* is the playfield, fenced by a set of principles, within which you apply emotional intelligence.

- Emotional intelligence involves recognizing emotions, developing an understanding of them, and managing them to everyone's advantage by building connections.

THE FUNDAMENTAL CONCEPTS
OF EMOTIONAL INTELLIGENCE

We are making good progress and moving forward. We've defined and compared the two key aspects we're discussing: the *Emotional Intelligence Theory* and the way to gain full advantage of it, which is through applying emotional intelligence.

We've established that to benefit from the *Emotional Intelligence Theory*, we must possess emotional intelligence. We've examined this idea from several perspectives, but now we need to dive in and clarify precisely what emotional intelligence is built upon.

There's a reason you have five fingers on your hand. It's because you will want to count the five concepts that go into emotional intelligence. So, let's go through them:

Foundations

These concepts are fundamental prerequisites for developing the capacity to understand and regulate yourself and connect meaningfully with others.

1.   **Self-awareness** – We will delve more deeply into self-awareness and all other concepts in the next parts of this book but suffice it to say that it all begins with understanding yourself. It's based on the principle that to understand and know others, you first need to understand and know yourself. A good definition of self-awareness is the understanding and recognition of your

own emotions AND (you must have known there was an 'and' making its way in) how your emotions affect your thoughts and behavior.

2. **Self-regulation** – Self-regulation must begin with a certain level of self-awareness, as noted on your scorecard. That's because it starts with self-knowledge and builds the ability to manage your emotions healthily, not letting your natural emotional tendencies take over. Emotions are good and bad, nice and not so nice, but what is bad is when your actions are dominated by how you feel. That sort of impulsiveness is never a good idea because it is incompatible with the principle of working cooperatively and interacting meaningfully with others. You must learn to regulate yourself to become emotionally intelligent.

3. **Empathy** – Empathy is about walking in the other person's shoes or seeing the world through their eyes and hearing the way they perceive things. Let's make the point by drawing a picture, not literally, of course. You might feel on top of the world about yourself, having completed self-awareness and self-regulation courses and emerged at the top of the class. You, therefore, know yourself and can regulate your emotions. But can you put yourself in the skin of someone with a different cultural background from yours? If you are from the United States, can you imagine what life looks like from a Chinese perspective? And, if Chinese, can you get inside the head of a Latin American? And can Latin Americans really understand how a US person feels? This is a game you can play with as many points and questions as there are cultures or personality types in the world. Empathy is a key requirement because it is the ability

to understand the thoughts, feelings, and emotions of others.

Adaptability

These concepts are ways to interact with others in a meaningful way.

4. **Psychological Intelligence** – Now, we move on to a part of emotional intelligence that we are all familiar with in concept, but don't necessarily call it psychological intelligence. More commonly, it is referred to as *reading others*, which is essentially the ability to understand how people react and behave in particular circumstances, as seen earlier. It's a bit like a science experiment with constants and variables. You have the constant being the situation, and the variable being the person. The key thing is that if you have psychological intelligence, you can read others and even make a good guess at how they are most likely to react.

5. **Emotional Agility** – Susan David is a psychologist and faculty member at Harvard Medical School. She developed and formalized the concept of *emotional agility* in her 2016 book, *Emotional Agility: Get Unstuck, Embrace Change, and Thrive in Work and Life.* The concept refers to navigating and responding effectively to our constantly shifting emotional states, with self-awareness and flexibility. In simple terms, it's about being able to tune in to the appropriate emotions to respond effectively to an interaction. It is a concept not too far from empathy. The more you understand that person's thoughts and feelings (*Psychological Intelligence*), the more you can adapt to them (*Emotional Agility*), to benefit from the best outcome.

Once you have integrated those concepts, which we will delve into in future chapters again, you are ready to interact using emotional intelligence.

The Pyramid Block Diagram below organizes these concepts in a more visual form:

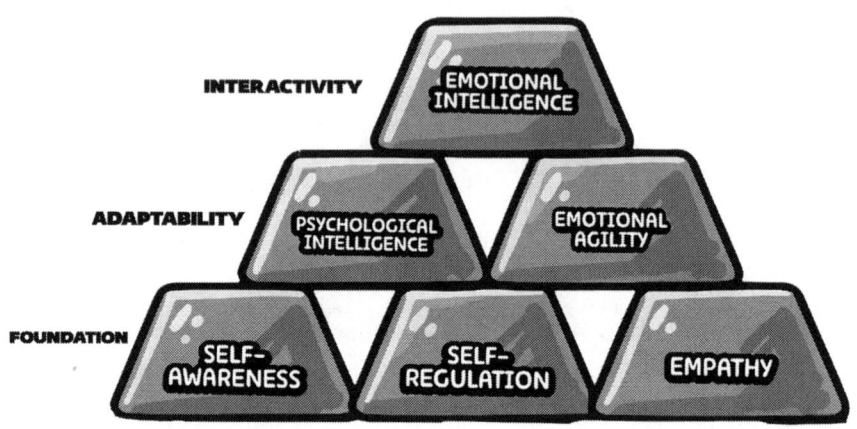

PART 2
SELF-AWARENESS

CHAPTER

3

SELF-AWARENESS: FIRST, KNOW YOURSELF

"Knowing yourself is the beginning of all wisdom."
— *Aristotle, ancient Greek philosopher*

AN INVITATION TO A SELF-AWARENESS TEST

Now, it is time to put the theory to one side and take a good (and honest) look at yourself. The key to accuracy in the personality tests that follow is to be intuitive in your answers. There are no right or wrong answers. If in doubt, don't overthink matters; answer on your gut instinct. Be spontaneous and see how you feel afterward.

The tests are both free and will take five minutes or more, depending on how much time you want to spend deliberating each question.

Note that this test has no affiliation with this book, its author, or the publishing company. They were hand-picked for their proven reliability.

16PERSONALITIES

Duration

This popular, user-friendly personality test incorporates a modern approach to the Myers-Briggs Type Indicator, a well-known personality assessment tool, helping you explore how you think, feel, and interact.

BIG FIVE

Duration

This comprehensive, highly recognized, research-backed psychological assessment measures five core traits: Extroversion, Emotional Stability, Agreeableness, Conscientiousness, and Intellect/Imagination.

Be honest and have fun!

UNDERSTANDING YOUR BEHAVIORAL PATTERNS

What was your personality type? Do you agree with it? If yes, read on. If not, consider whether you were sincere in your answers. Remember, this is about who you are and not how you think other people see you or how you want to be seen.

Often, with these tests, you will find that they are only 80-90% accurate. Therefore, it is essential to remember that accuracy is not the most critical factor, but rather the hints they provide toward triggers for improvement.

Whatever your personality type, you will find that you have strengths, areas for development, and blind spots, along with suggested career paths, as outlined by the 16personalities test. Whether the recommendation is for you to become a scientist carrying out research into obscure forms of bacteria (love of attention to detail, facts and discovery, along with a clinical organized approach to a working day), or a clown actor entertaining at kids' birthday parties (never happier than with an audience, ad-libbing through life and bringing laughter and joy to everyone), you're going to get some strong personality traits and some areas that might need attention.

However, the key thing to bear in mind is that everyone is different, and a particular trait like being decisive doesn't necessarily put that person at the top of the ladder. This is an exercise in getting to know yourself, not some grand scheme to rank everybody like a football league. In fact, one person's strength may well be another's weakness. There are no good or bad traits. It is situational. Only situations reveal the trait as a strength or a weakness. It is science, as far as psychology is concerned. But not mathematics, with right and wrong answers. Good or bad traits. This is just an excellent way to explore oneself a little further.

Let's look at the strengths. These should resonate with you enormously. They did when I took the test, but I had to remind myself to follow the rules first, although there is only one rule—be honest.

Human nature is what it is; we know the extremes of our personalities better than we think we do. We know if we're a party animal or a poet at heart. Thus, we will recognize both strengths and weaknesses, which might make us smile as our characters are revealed on the screen.

We might not like the areas highlighted for development, but we must remember the cardinal rule concerning honesty. Knowing these areas where you might need to improve is much more constructive for our self-development than praising ourselves for our apparent strengths.

Building a fully efficient leadership personality involves identifying areas for improvement and transforming them into strengths.

However, the primary goal is not to act upon areas of improvement immediately or implement radical actions. Being aware naturally brings in self-regulation with it.

4

FEEDBACK: THE GIFT MOST LEADERS AVOID

> *"Feedback is the breakfast of champions."*
> — *Ken Blanchard, author of the One Minute Manager*

HOW TO INVITE AND RECEIVE HONEST FEEDBACK

You've probably bumped into a 'present recycler' at one point or another. These people accept presents in the usual way, uttering the required 'what an imaginative idea,' before putting it in a department of their mind that deals with whom it might be passed on to; an agile mind can quickly distil the possibilities to form a short list. On the next birthday, the present recycler-turned-giver gets the same comments as 'what an imaginative idea.'

Very often, books are read and digested before being passed on. Provided the original recipient is careful, who will ever know?

'Yes,' you think, 'I know several people who fit the bill, some not even bothering to keep the book looking new, but what relevance does this have on feedback?'

Well, feedback is a gift. It might not come wrapped in Christmas paper, but it's still a gift. In fact, feedback is a truly valuable gift that keeps on giving, much like the gym subscription your favorite aunt forgets to cancel month after month and year after year.

Feedback shares its usefulness with a 'present recycler' in another distinct way because someone who receives feedback from their boss, mentor, or any reliable source, and accepts it openly, grows as a result. That puts them in the strongest position to give feedback to those who report to them. In this way, feedback is capable of expanding and helping many others, causing a kind of appraisal chain that extends down through generations, much like the ripple effect of buying coffee forward.

So, how does one manage this feedback, considering that most people avoid it as much as possible? The answer to that question is to treat it as the asset it is. That translates into listening, thinking, and then deciding what you can do to make improvements.

The challenge comes in not rejecting it (unless, of course, it's deliberately not helpful in the first place, which does happen from time to time). Here are some steps to aid in the process:

- Consider that all feedback is valuable, and you can select what to keep for later.

- Listen attentively during the feedback session and digest the information later.

- Make notes, if not at the meeting, immediately afterward.

- Try to condense it down into key points. What is essential, and what falls into the incidental column?

- Finally, come up with a plan by extracting the key actions from the points you've come up with.

- Well, not quite finally, because the real final thing is to follow up and ensure that the action plan is taking shape and that improvements are made.

Remember, the point of all this is for you to grow as an individual, which will translate to both your work and personal life. As a leader, you can recycle the gift of feedback, knowing that those you help will, in turn, help others.

What you shouldn't do, however, and that many people do regardless, is to receive feedback, dislike it (often because it holds a profound truth you hate), lurk and pass it on, as a form of revenge for having been the recipient in the first place.

Many people receive formal appraisals as part of their employment. Students get a rundown of their arguments and ideas every time their tutor reviews their latest essay. Musicians and comedians gauge their success by the volume of applause after a performance.

Alternatively, you can seek feedback from multiple sources, such as family members, friends, and work colleagues. It's pretty normal to want to know how you're doing, but taking in their observations can sometimes be a little intimidating, which can hurt your pride and ego; hence, it's often avoided.

And this is where a key factor comes in. To be the best you can be at whatever you do, you need a growth mindset, which includes the ability to receive feedback, so never turn your back on it, however hurtful it may be.

Treat everyone's comments as a key way forward. You seek honest opinions on how you are doing, and the most honest views are often the hardest to bear. This is to help your journey, not necessarily to determine whether the feedback giver genuinely likes you or not. That almost doesn't matter.

I'm sure you've heard the phrase, 'You have to be cruel to be kind.' It needs adaptation to fit into feedback mode, so perhaps you could say, 'You have to be straight with the truth to be of true benefit to those around you.'

Think of a genuine feedback process as a contract. Let's give an example. You're a student and have written an essay on some obscure philosophy section. You hand in your final version and are pretty pleased with the result. A countdown starts when you get your tutor's opinion. Finally, the appointed hour arrives, and you knock on her door, determined not to show your nerves.

Let's follow through the process with a series of options:

a) The tutor is highly critical of the essay. This could be because (i) it is genuinely dreadful, or (ii) you've got better ideas than your tutor and he's mad at you because he believes he's being upstaged.

b) The tutor is full of praise. This could be because (i) it really is excellent, or (ii) your tutor only skim-reads moments before your meeting, and they think praise will cover the omission.

c) The tutor makes a mix of thoughtful comments and valid criticisms. In other words, they have read it, thought about it, and found the time to scribble down some good points for improvement.

Now, if I ask you which option you think is the most positive and helpful in progressing your ability to reason, argue, and state your case, and you reply either (a) or (b), I have to say you may need to read again the first part of this chapter.

There is another type of feedback where the identity of the person who made the comments is unknown. If you've ever operated a suggestion box, after playing the game of guessing who made which suggestion, you will notice that some are thoughtful and constructive, while others are sarcastic or downright silly. Those you quickly put aside, not wasting any more time on them. The positive pile, however, is something you want to take a few minutes to absorb and reflect on, remembering that these are constructive opinions from people who know the business well.

And who would not want to make the best of every opportunity by listening to the reflections of others who will see the world slightly differently from you?

The 360-degree feedback method, which falls under the category of anonymous and extremely constructive feedback, is a survey sent to your colleagues, direct reports, and supervisors that asks insightful questions about how they perceive your leadership style. The result is a comprehensive report with anonymous input covering the broad scope of common leadership traits.

For the results to be meaningful and impactful, the survey should include at least:

- Two employees from your team
- Two colleagues with no reporting lines to you
- Your direct manager
- And optionally, two people from your personal life

And of course, the more the merrier. Because the feedback is anonymous, it is supposedly candid, and you will get a more realistic representation of how others perceive you, which can reveal insights you may not have considered.

You may try the following 360 tool, which is a free solution and requires a simple registration and don't forget to let your manager, selected peers, employees, family, and friends know that you are taking this initiative and that the survey is 100% anonymous, which will allow them to provide input as honestly as possible.

Scan and Register

Feedback should always be taken seriously when it's seriously intended. It's another view on the world that can only help you become better at what you do. This leads us nicely onto the next section of this chapter.

TURNING CRITICISM INTO POSITIVE AWARENESS

"I know I've got an odd name, but then I am pretty different, you know. What's my name? Dr.Genuis, you've probably heard of me. But if it makes it easier, you can call me 'The Doctor.' I got top marks in my Chemistry PhD, and I'm looking forward to moving through the ranks of Chem Inc on my way to the top. 'I'll give it about five years, and you'll be on the board,' my mentor at Harvard said and..."

This may be an exaggeration, but the caricature makes the point.

Oversized egos have no place in the modern workplace. It delays progress. Everybody has an ego, of course, but the oversized variety causes problems. Do you remember the old saying of pride before a fall? Well, that's precisely what happened to Dr. Genius (who is not leading with emotional intelligence, I guarantee you). The sad thing is he brought it on himself because he brushed aside all the valid points made in his formal appraisals, just as he refused to listen to the casual, friendly advice from the senior colleague at Chem Inc.

Even his kind-hearted assistant tried, in her gentle way, to point out that the world of work was a place of learning and development for those open enough to listen and learn.

One way of looking at it is to say there are two types of people in this modern world. There are those who listen and those who don't. This is very categorical, I know, but also very accurate in the world of emotional intelligence, and wild statements are often based on fundamental truths. This is no exception. If you want to become an intelligent leader, you need to develop enough humility to listen to feedback about your performance and decipher it, distilling it into a plan to develop yourself. It's called embracing feedback, adopting humility, and accepting criticism alongside the praise everyone seeks.

But fundamentally, it's about listening, thinking about what you've heard, then listening and thinking some more.

How often have you heard someone coming out of an appraisal meeting all hot under the collar, indignance lacing their words when they state, "What does he know about selling techniques and customer reassurance? Isn't he the one who froze at that big conference last year? You know, we lost the contract with XYZ Inc. as a result."

Let's replay that, concentrating on the background of your angry statement, but doing it with an open mind and a generous heart.

In other words, rather than getting hot under the collar, let's keep calm and use our emotional intelligence to gain from a minimum of empathy.

First, you've not been with the business since it started, not even since your boss joined, so what do you know about his achievements? Perhaps he froze when speaking about the contract for an entirely different reason from the generally accepted one, namely that he panicked when the customer needed reassurance that the contract was in hand.

Second, perhaps the contract wasn't in hand, and your boss was just being open about dealing with a difficult situation. Maybe the customer appreciated that honesty but had to cancel despite it because the top-level contract with their customer was put on hold.

You can already see that it's essential for any empathetic individual to have a distinct understanding that humility is a powerful and positive quality.

Furthermore, humility and confidence often walk hand in hand. If you're genuinely open to improvement as a person, you will grow enormously and naturally in confidence. In contrast, people often use arrogance and pride to mask a lack of confidence.

It's nice to know that when you stand tall, you've got honesty and openness right beside you.

Third, and final, if all the points were as the rumors stated, meaning that everything about your manager was true, that doesn't mean the points he raised don't apply to you. No 'performance whitewash' is available that says if you can find even the tiniest fault in what your boss says, everything else he comes up with can safely be ignored. This isn't the case of flashing the get-out-of-jail-free card you've got tucked up your sleeve:

He was wrong about something once.

Therefore,

He must always be wrong now.

Therefore,

I don't need to listen to him.

Well, that must be just about the worst argument ever to grace the corporate world. It lacks all logic. Let's look, instead, at a more reasoned approach:

He was wrong about the deal with that German company.

However,

That doesn't mean he's always wrong.

In fact,

He may have learned from his mistakes and totally reworked the whole procedure.

Therefore,

I need to listen to him and give him the benefit of the doubt.

I'm good at making final points to add as an appendix to my previous final point, but bear with me a moment longer because there is one more final point to make on the subject of listening to feedback and really taking in what people are saying.

What if your boss really did freeze at the conference last year because he couldn't think how to respond to the customer assurance demands of the firm's biggest customer? Instead of denying him the right to comment on your performance now, might it not actually add a new weight to the advice he now offers you?

This person has experienced the dread of freezing in front of a senior corporate audience. Maybe his experience speaks volumes about his warning to you.

In other words, just as they say you learn more from your mistakes than your successes, maybe there's a way for the open-minded to learn from the mistakes of others.

All it takes is openness, a desire to improve, and the willingness to learn from others.

And a hefty dose of humility.

Summary

- Feedback is a gift you can both give and receive.

- Feedback opens the door of self-awareness, which, if adequately treated, leads to personal growth.

- Feedback also forms a chain that keeps growing because you get better at giving constructive feedback yourself, developing your leadership.

- Feedback must lead to a plan of improvement at some point, otherwise it fades away into the mist of, 'didn't somebody once point that out to me?'

- Feedback can be direct (from your manager) or anonymous (as in suggestion boxes). Unless it is offered with malice, it's always useful.

- Feedback can lead to awareness through listening, taking to heart, and planning for improvement.

- Finally, loop back to the top and read again that feedback is a gift you can both give and receive. So, be generous with yourself and others.

BUILDING PERSONAL GROWTH THROUGH FEEDBACK

In 2014, the world changed. At least it did for the tens of thousands of Microsoft employees in Redmond, Washington, where Microsoft Headquarters is located. That was the year Satya Nadella, a long-term employee at Microsoft, was made Chief Executive Officer.

So, why the change?

Mr. Nadella, taking over from Steve Ballmer, inherited from Mr. Ballmer's stake ranking system, which implied ranking employees against each other, with an imposed proportion of employees ranked as poor performers and another proportion as high achievers, fostering a culture of internal competition, individualism, and corporate politics.

Upon being appointed CEO, Mr. Nadella introduced a new approach to doing business, one that emphasizes an empathy-driven culture. He aimed to cultivate a 'growth mindset' among Microsoft employees, which he achieved by integrating every aspect of emotional intelligence into the core of the Microsoft culture and operation, including fostering inclusion and encouraging everyone to contribute.

Interestingly, the first step in his thought process was self-awareness, recognizing that Microsoft's culture was centered on the wrong values, such as self-centered departments and a lack of recognition for team achievements, which overemphasized individual achievements instead. By recognizing it, he and, by extension, Microsoft, became aware of their weaknesses, and the awareness served as a springboard for improvement.

He then implemented annual employee engagement surveys, collaboration metrics as part of the key performance indicators (KPIs), and performance reviews with 360-degree feedback, encouraging frequent check-ins between managers and staff, realizing that one time a year was not frequent enough to build a relationship of trust and nurture skills.

An interesting point, because many people recognize that a year is a long time in business, as it is in a working career. Relying on a single annual appraisal meeting considerably slows down the benefits of feedback and improvement, which greatly interests the Empathic manager.

During the more frequent meetings of minds between a manager and someone reporting to them, Satya encouraged a novel approach. The feedback points were not filed away to be dragged out again moments before the next meeting. Instead, the employee was to use them to develop an action plan or improvement plan, while these points were still fresh in mind, and the manager and employee were together.

Thus, it became a joint plan, owned by both parties, with both parties invested in the plan, to become more productive, measurable, and achievable than ever before.

It might be easier to break this rapid process into three key stages. For simplicity's sake, we will refer to them as Assessment, Commitment, and Tracking, or ACT, although that is an oversimplification of the processes involved:

The 'A'

This involves listening, meditating, clarifying, and analyzing. It might start with a few observation points, where employees reflect on why they acted in specific ways. They may have some questions to clarify certain aspects before proceeding with the assessment of strengths and weaknesses exhibited.

The 'C'

The 'A' slides neatly into this section because the assessment highlights key points where improvement can be made. This might be ways to educate and learn, different approaches to employ, or even alternative behavior to adopt. Hence, we are creating an action plan consisting of a short number of achievable and measurable steps for improvement. There is no point in having too many because the lack of concentration will be overwhelming.

The 'T'

Tracking means resurrecting the old plan from the previous session and examining what went well and what went poorly. Perhaps 70% of the points raised last time were achieved, leaving 30% to be incorporated into the continuous improvement plan.

That would still mean a significant achievement.

The *ACT method* demonstrates the positive effect of frequent, informal feedback sessions, leading to rapid action plans. This approach enables us to avoid waiting for the next annual appraisal and then struggling to recall what was discussed last time. It also fosters a more genuine and caring employee relationship, given the regularity of the feedback sessions.

Considering that it is not always easy to provide feedback to others, here is a list covering what can go wrong during the feedback sessions and what we can do about it.

Challenges	Context	Best Practices
Overemphasis on Weaknesses	Probably the most common. Managers come up with what they have to say, often biased opinions, and forget to emphasize the positive aspect of someone's performance as well.	**Always start with the positive.** Mean what you say. Be constructive.
Lack of Clarity	The feedback is opinion-based and highly subjective. It lacks facts.	**Always be objective.** State a concrete example. Always propose a constructive way forward.
Emotional Reactions	The employees become upset and start responding negatively.	**Always stay calm.** Listen and acknowledge how they feel. Keep the tone collaborative.
Manager Discomfort	You avoid feedback or downplay what should be said.	**Always be prepared.** Focus on growth, not on judgments.
Misalignment on Expectations	Your employees have a different understanding of what is expected of them than you do.	**Always be clear with your expectations.** Clarify the employee's role, responsibility, and objectives.
Lack of Listening	You are not taking into account your employees' input.	**Always make the session a two-way street.** Ask open questions.
Poor Timing	The feedback session is done at the wrong time or in the wrong context.	**Always be sensitive to 'the best moment.'** Think about the best moment to put chances of success on your side.
No Follow-Up	The feedback session concludes without an action plan or agreed-upon follow-up.	**Always with the next steps.** Summarize agreed actions, timing, and resources.

Take a moment to examine the solutions. They have an emphasized rule, which, if followed, guarantees success. You will also notice that most of them focus on emotional intelligence.

Anybody can achieve emotional intelligence. It might help if you are fit and well, but it is primarily a state of mind.

A compassionate state of mind.

CHAPTER SUMMARY:
RECEIVING & PROCESSING FEEDBACK

We've reached the end of another chapter, one that concerns feedback and how individuals can utilize it. We've considered that feedback can be both constructive and negative. Negative feedback can stem from a series of darker emotions, such as envy and apathy, or frustrations; it often involves unbalanced opinions, in the worst case, even sarcasm, and should be ignored.

Positive feedback arises from a genuine desire to help and assist. It works through openness and honesty and therefore has a raw power that is hard to deny.

We've looked at feedback from the perspective of it being an unwelcome gift, something to avoid at all costs, shunting it across our minds into the reject department, which is by definition against the concept of a growth mindset. Yet, constructive feedback is the opposite, building on praise and criticism (that criticism is gentle like the rain), because it helps us move forward.

And, as we move forward, we take others with us, just as others have brought us along with them. Thus, it becomes a chain of improvement and hope, just like buying coffee forward.

Even within this, we've discussed how everybody has weaknesses. However, weaknesses can be turned into positives because, as humans, we tend to learn more from failure than from success. It's just the way we are and how the world is. Humans often talk of the roses of success rising from the ashes of disaster. We need to cultivate a growth mindset.

Then, we examined the remarkable 'revolution' that Satya Nadella has instigated at Microsoft, simply by promoting the concept of a growth mindset based on the principles of emotional intelligence. However, ever aware of human failure, we've examined common problems that managers encounter when giving feedback to their employees, which, by the way, apply very well in your personal life as well. We have observed that these trends share common themes centered on emotional intelligence and how feedback is supported by several principles, which, if applied, can be powerful and enhance your feedback sessions. This is emotional intelligence in action.

PART 3
SELF-REGULATION

CHAPTER

5

RECOGNIZING YOUR TENDENCIES

*"The greatest ability in business is to get along with others
and influence their actions."*
*— John Hancock, U.S. Founding Father and signatory of
the Declaration of Independence*

IDENTIFY AND REGULATE YOUR TENDENCIES

John Hancock lived from 1737 to 1793 and, as well as his elaborate signature on the Declaration of Independence, from which the phrase 'put your John Hancock on the document' comes, he was also a successful businessman and politician, becoming one of the wealthiest men in America. He was also part of a loose group of merchants and businessmen who dominated much of the Atlantic trade in the second half of the 18th Century.

He stands out for another reason, one that I believe underpinned his business success, and this is encapsulated in the quotation above:

> *The greatest ability in business is to get along with others and influence their actions.*

While the concept of self-awareness dates back to some of the earliest philosophers, such as Socrates and Aristotle, they weren't generally involved in commerce. John Hancock represents an early devotee and advocate of the power of emotional intelligence in the business world. He had a vast network of contacts, mainly because he had the empathy to understand their position rather than riding roughshod over anybody who got in his way.

If you want an example of how not to develop emotional intelligence, I suggest looking at fiction and settling on Logan Roy, in Succession, a critically acclaimed television drama series.

Alright, we recognize the value of emotional intelligence in both business and non-business settings. It's a positive, mindful way to take people with you. And, on the basis that two minds are better than one, it stands to reason that if you can take the whole department with you, you are far better off than trying to handle your objectives alone or forcing others to move forward. But why is self-awareness the first step to emotional intelligence?

To understand that, we must remind ourselves what emotional intelligence is. It's an awareness of other people, specifically how their emotions influence their behavior, as well as how your own emotions govern your behavior. It is a language. A language that you first need to talk to connect.

When inner selves meet, we can't use sight for obvious reasons. In fact, we can't use any of the traditional senses. Instead, we utilize the concept known as emotional intelligence. And the better we understand our inner self, the more we can explore that of others.

Imagine an arm-wrestling contest where you want to match your strength with your opponent's. You must first know your strength. So, it is with your emotions and your inner self. The more you know about yourself, the more you can understand others. Thankfully, emotional intelligence is a much gentler language.

There's another reason why self-awareness is the first step. That's because self-regulation is the second step. Again, the arm-wrestling scenario comes to mind. If you don't know your strength, how can you hope to control it during the contest?

Therefore, there is self-awareness of who we are and what our natural tendencies are. And there are ways to regulate our emotions. Interestingly, knowing who we are and our natural tendencies is already a way to control them. Imagine now an emotional dashboard. So, think about your car. Of course, every model is different, but each has a dashboard littered with switches, levers, and dials.

It's the dials we are most interested in. These give us a visual representation of our emotional state. On one side are our natural tendencies, and above each of them are dials that move up or down depending on the situation we are facing. The goal is to ensure that these natural tendencies are monitored and compensated for, so they never exceed a certain level.

Knowing your emotions and how they regulate throughout various situations is, in effect, a part of the necessary self-awareness needed to best reflect on and improve over time. The dashboard helps us visualize the concept.

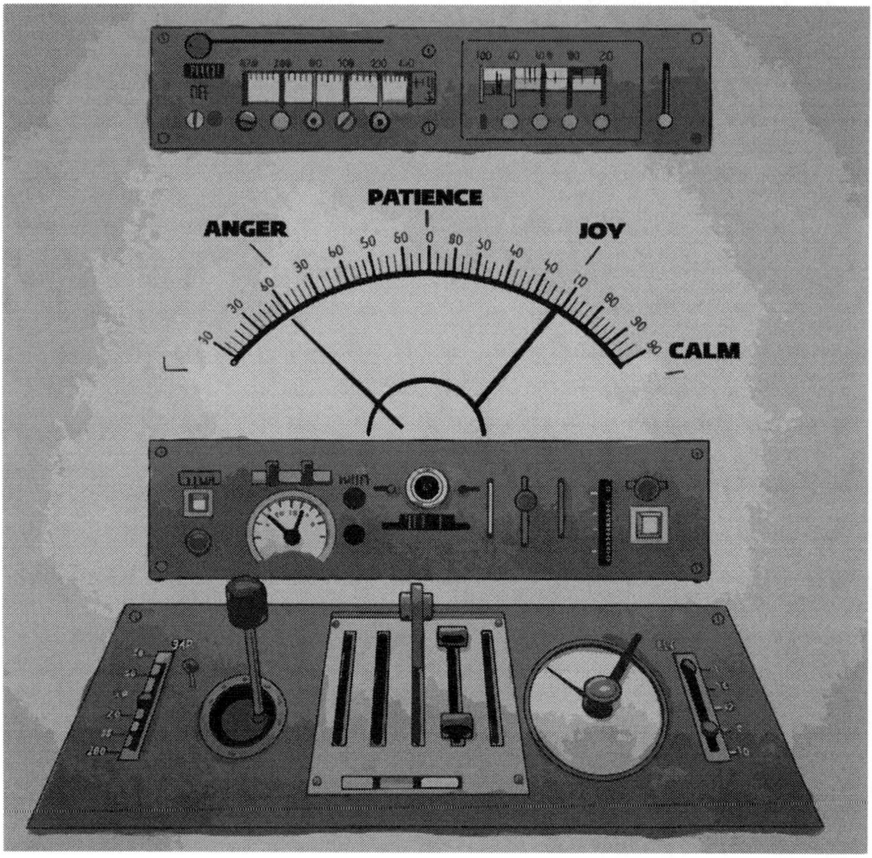

There are also journaling methods, such as a document where we would enter information about our mood, the emotions we are feeling, their extent, and when they occur. The journal then transforms this information into a neat display of how we feel, from the inside out.

To summarize, understanding our tendencies and emotional state helps us regulate or compensate for them, ensuring we never reach the red mark on the dial and maintain a state where we are in control and can interact with others most constructively.

Now, we're getting to the crunch on this concept. If we know how to control ourselves, we are already halfway there; the missing part is reading and understanding another person, perhaps someone who works for us or to whom we report, which we will explore in a future chapter covering psychological intelligence. This concept will help us read others' tendencies during a negotiation and seek ways to meet them halfway.

We're referring to tendencies such as motivation, stress levels, impatience, confidence, and even communication methods. These are all things that John Hancock would have approved of in terms of investing time to understand. After all, if you can understand what stresses someone out or what drives them to compete, you can progress the desired deal because you know how to react to their needs or fears.

In summary:

- In business, getting along with others gives you an edge because it allows you to connect.

- Emotional intelligence is a positive and mindful way to take people with you.

- Self-awareness and self-regulation are closely linked because knowing yourself is essential to regulating yourself efficiently.

- There are ways to visualize and remain intentionally aware of our current state, allowing us to know ourselves and regulate our emotions.

RECOGNIZING THE SIGNS THAT
LEAD TO OVERREACTION

Let's start with a recap. We're working together through the steps to emotional intelligence, recognizing that this is a key pillar to efficiently applying the *Emotional Intelligence Theory*. We've established that self-awareness is step number one, followed by self-regulation. We then looked at the emotional dashboard, that extraordinary interactive collection of data on our emotional makeup, which is more fascinating by far than any ordinary computer game because it deals with real people coping with real people.

And it does not stop when we shake hands. Instead, it continues until we evolve and explore, until we've a solid understanding of the inner self.

But wait a minute, aren't we just playing with information? Should we not delve beneath the dials to find out how the engine affects our motoring performance?

Yes, and that is precisely what we will do right now. We're going to look at triggers. We're not going hunting, but we're looking for something very similar to that slow, cool pressure of the finger on the trigger.

We are examining the factors that contribute to these tendencies. In other words, what causes overreactions? Why is that sales manager so ambitious? Why does the financial controller avoid direct contact and only communicate by email?

Before we plough into this, however, let's take another step backward or sideways. What we want to do is step out of the scene for a minute and remind ourselves why we're doing this.

We know that the natural tendencies tend to be negative or "too much." If we burrow down far enough, we can determine what causes them to surface. Then, we can take action to address the issue.

Self-regulation with a strong accent on the 'self.' It all starts with you.

The trouble is, this requires consistent effort, but the rewards are well worth it. How do we identify the triggers within our emotions? The first part of the answer may frustrate you because I must remind you that each person is unique. Hence, you need to find them on your own.

This is why self-awareness is critical, which is also why we started with the personality tests earlier.

There is a misconception that practice makes perfect, which is wrong.

Self-reflection and growing awareness breed improvement, and thus, perfection over time. Sure, you need to practice, but if it isn't paired with conscious self-reflection and other methods to cultivate awareness, practice may only yield mediocre outcomes.

In addition to the tests, we will cover some guidance that should push you in a particular direction. The guidance shows a combination of the different techniques to grow awareness of your tendencies, and it's up to you to determine which ones work best for you. So, here goes:

1. **Self-reflection** – You knew it was coming, didn't you? This process is similar to how an analyst considers a problem to derive a solution. Think about yourself, how others perceive you, your tendencies, and what powerful emotional reactions you've experienced over time, and why they happened. The self-awareness test in the earlier chapter is a good way to know yourself better. Recognizing your tendencies and triggers is essential. Then, learning how to regulate them.

2. **Emotional audit** – If you wanted to be scientific, you could do this at set times a day and record the results like you were taking a psychology class. Other people might be more relaxed, asking

themselves how they are feeling from time to time. Similar to self-regulation, you're looking for patterns. Do you always feel good in the morning and low after lunch? Are you better with the routine of a working day rather than the freedom the weekend offers?

3. **Feedback** – As seen in Chapter 4, another old chestnut that comes up time and again. However, this isn't so much about formal appraisals; it is about getting input from friends and family regarding your reaction to particular events. For instance, after a row at the car hire company, you might ask your friend or colleague how they thought you handled yourself. Just go a little deeper than 'you did fine,' because you want to learn about yourself, and your reactions to external events are key. The 360-degree feedback for that effect is an excellent tool for collecting feedback and growing awareness.

4. **Mindfulness** – This can help you recognize your current emotions and focus on what triggers them. You won't reach a state of self-awareness and self-regulation through mindfulness alone, but it is a valuable addition to your "know yourself" toolkit. This could be a result of meditation or engaging in creative activities, such as writing stories, composing songs, or drawing. It could also come from yoga or simply walking while you think. It's about being present in the moment and aware of what's happening.

You will also experiment with other techniques that may prove helpful. One key aspect is keeping a journal so you can record the different results from the various tracking you want to follow up on. Don't worry if you find one technique that leaves you unimpressed. Remember, this is a deeply personal thing, and everyone is different. You need to find techniques to determine your emotional triggers. At that point, you are well on the way to self-regulation.

So, what are we saying? We're talking about triggers and discussing that:

- Natural tendencies tend to be negative, such as impatience, stress, and fear, leading to an excess of attitude and unfavorable outcomes.

- It's vital to be able to recognize the triggers to these natural tendencies and regulate ourselves before or when they kick in.

- To self-regulate, we need to understand the emotions we feel, and the triggers behind these emotions are important because they govern our behavior.

- We find these triggers through self-reflection, emotional audits, feedback, and mindfulness exercises.

BREAKING FREE FROM AUTOMATIC
RESPONSES AND NEGATIVE TENDENCIES

Why are there so many expressions for when something gets on your nerves? Let's play a game where we shout out one thing, each person in turn. The first one to not have a saying drops out, and the last person standing is the winner.

I start with 'he drives me up the wall.' Within minutes, we also have:

She really gets on my wick

He's getting under my skin

She's making my blood boil

He's really testing my patience

I'm sure you got the message. The point is that we've let the side down when we start splashing these clichés around.

We are following an established pattern that starts with an automatic response. That's not good when you consider an awful lot more can be done through cooperation than antagonism.

Let's take a different approach and revisit the past, reliving the mood and feelings we experienced at the trigger point. There was a situation, and we reacted negatively to it. We followed a negative tendency. The result could be catastrophic. In personal terms, it could be a broken relationship or an abandoned friendship. In work terms, it could lead to the resignation of a valued employee or the loss of a key contract.

In this situation, we have self-awareness and self-regulation on one side and natural tendencies and automatic responses on the other. Between these are the triggers, which can fire in either direction. Left alone, we humans tend to follow our natural tendency, because unfortunately, they are much easier to embrace. It takes a great deal of presence of mind and strength of character to buck the trend and forge a different route forward.

That can only happen when we get to know ourselves.

Remember that words carry great power. With words, you can express love, just as much as you can hurt someone so profoundly that they may never recover from the internal bleed. Language is a powerful tool to be used with care.

Now, all is not lost, because there are other tools you can use when you feel yourself on the slippery slope toward a natural reaction. Let's finish this chapter with a look at some of these:

i. **Take a step backward** – The origin of this phrase must come from stepping back from the point of confrontation, but nowadays it means any way in which we step back before that trigger is pressed.

ii.   **Be reflective** – A similar concept where we withdraw and think things through, asking, 'Do I really want to go down that route?' Usually, this might involve reflection in a quiet and calming place, embracing silence because it helps concentration on what really matters.

iii.   **Think strategically**, with pragmatism and analysis – Both of these can head off those automatic responses before they cause the damage you really don't want to happen.

The common factor among those methods is regulation. You must regulate yourself to get the best out of situations involving others.

CHAPTER SUMMARY: RECOGNIZING YOUR TENDENCIES

It seems a long time ago that we stepped ashore in Boston Harbor to shake hands with John Hancock. He seemed to be the living embodiment of emotional intelligence with a vast network of contacts and friends across business and politics, which he managed with high emotional awareness.

John knew that people reacted differently to the same events. That's because, thank goodness, we are all different. He took the trouble to know himself so that he could know others.

We have established during this chapter that the first step is knowing yourself, and the second one is self-regulation, because self-regulation is only possible if we first know ourselves. Then, we examined ways to remain aware of our emotions.

From the emotional dashboard, it's a simple step to look below dials and levers and determine that there are these things called natural tendencies—how we naturally react without any higher-level input from our self-regulated self. We examined the types of natural tendencies before moving on to the triggers that activate these automatic reactions.

Finally, we concluded with a look at some of the tools we can use to manage these natural tendencies and automatic reactions, reminding ourselves that we do this because we want to achieve the best outcomes for people at an emotional level. In the next chapter, we will deepen this understanding.

That's the route to understanding the *Emotional Intelligence Theory*.

CHAPTER

6

STAYING IN CONTROL

> *"The most difficult thing is the decision to act; the rest is merely tenacity. The fears are paper tigers. You can do anything you decide to do. You can act to change and control your life; and the procedure, the process is its own reward."*
> – Amelia Earhart, U.S. flight pioneer

STEP BACK: HOW TO RESET UNDER PRESSURE

Things go wrong in life, whether at work, rest, or play. If it were possible to control everything that ever happens, we would live in a sublime but boring world. Luckily, we do not. However, that means there will be situations that rapidly get out of control, and we need to know how to react to bring them back under at least some form of control.

This is where an old friend comes in, and that is self-regulation. Remember, we defined self-regulation as the ability to manage your emotions healthily. It's based on self-awareness to the point where you cannot properly self-regulate unless you have achieved a high level of self-awareness. It's like trying to build a house without pouring the foundations.

To self-regulate effectively, you must have a solid understanding of yourself as a foundation. Then, strong with the knowledge of who and what you are, there are strategies you can follow when the going gets tough.

Say you work for a newspaper. Sales of paper copies are dropping by the week; advertising revenue follows a similar pattern, with the trend line heading for disaster. The one saving grace is the website, where you're ahead of the rivals because your reporters have a nose for a good story. Your job is chief website editor; you've worked your way up to this senior position because you're good, but also because you've taken the time to work out where your strengths and weaknesses are and how they fit into the world of work.

You have a great network of journalists worldwide. You can rely on them, only this time, you can't, and the crash is spectacular. Joe Pascotti in Rome got it all wrong, and the pope isn't resigning because of scandal; he comes up smelling of roses, and you've got nothing to hit the headlines with.

You need a headline, and you've got a deadline. What do you do because you feel that rising panic is building up once again?

Well, as you know yourself, you've got some options. You know, in the back of your head, you've stored some stories for a rainy day. All you need to do is select one and expand on it.

But with four hours to go? And you know you tend to get hopelessly involved in the details. Left to your own devices, you'll happily spend three hours fifty on clarifying some points and then miss the deadline because there's no copy ready.

You sit down. You call a meeting in five minutes. You feel another rise of panic because, in five minutes, you must have your act together. Everything is conspiring against you. Is this some evil plot to get you fired? You catch yourself looking around at your team, wondering who has the ambition to take on your job, especially with all the pressure it entails.

Then, you close your eyes and spend three of the remaining four minutes in a meditative pose on the floor of your office. You can do this; you know you can. You know yourself, you know your team. There is a way around this.

"Are you coming, boss?" Fiona pokes her head around the door, breaking into your meditation. "I'm sorry, boss, I didn't realize you were meditating."

"Don't worry, Fi," you say, holding out a hand so she can pull you up. "Say, Fi, how do you feel about writing the text for today's story? You have a different writing style from mine, so I will want to review it carefully. However, you write much more quickly than I do. We're going to discuss the subject at this meeting, but can you then write a story in two hours?"

"Sure, I'd be delighted to do it, boss. But what will you be doing?"

"Once we have the subject, I'm going to work the rest to death with all the background stories. We're going to have a great set of stories, the best ever."

"I agree, boss, but aren't we putting the cart before the horse? I mean, we haven't even got a story yet."

"What about how the newspaper industry copes with pressure? You know, deadlines and all that."

"Perfect." Fi laughed. "Now come along, or you'll be late for your own meeting."

You faced a panic situation, yet despite cohabiting with fear, you didn't give way to it. Instead, you leveraged your self-awareness, combined with the strengths and weaknesses of your department, to devise a solution. You even had a chance to take a few precious minutes and reset your fevered mind through meditation. Your natural tendencies might have led you to stomp out of the newsroom, shouting that nobody could get the paper out of the mess that Joe Pascotti got you into.

Instead, you regrouped and devised a plan that matched everyone's strengths.

You did a good job because you could.

Let's have a look at ways to regulate when the pressure is high:

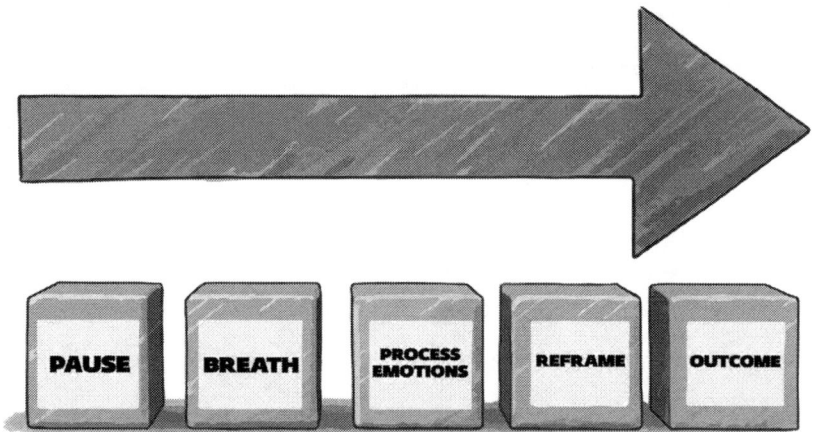

PAUSE – As seen earlier, stepping back is your best ally because you can't say or do anything wrong if you don't say or do anything. People usually like and give more importance to considered words.

BREATH – It may sound obvious, but stress and impulsions have as many mental signs as physical signs, and the best way to keep yourself grounded, in your best disposition, is to relax, regardless of the difficulty of the interaction.

PROCESS EMOTIONS – This means 'naming the emotions,' which is proven to reduce emotional weight and intensity. Ask yourself: What am I feeling right now? Give your emotions a name: anger, frustration, fear, or any other suitable feeling.

REFRAME – Put a definition to the current situation. Ask yourself:

WHO	*Who is involved?* *Who should be involved?*
WHAT	*What is at stake?* *What do the people involved want?*
WHEN	*When is the right moment to respond, or step back?* *When was the last time I felt like this before?*
WHY	*Why might the people involved behave this way?* *Why am I reacting this way?*
HOW	*How would I respond if I were at my best right now?* *How can I speak or act in a way I'll be proud of later?*

Answering these types of questions helps you set the parameters for your decisions.

OUTCOME – Emotionally Intelligent people focus on the outcome, not the impulse. Focus on what matters, keeping yourself grounded in pragmatism, so that you can act in a way that is true to your values and that you will be proud of.

Summary:

- Life can throw a lot of curveballs; the important thing is to stay in control.

- If you know your strengths and recognize your weaknesses, you're off to a flying start and are much more likely to stay in control than descend into panic.

- Once you know yourself, you can get to know others on an emotional level—this gives you an enhanced capability to make a sound plan.

- The outcome of a situation is more important than how you feel about it.

BREATHING, REFRAMING, AND REDIRECTING ENERGY

Our friend the news editor did a good job of turning things around, but sometimes a good job isn't quite enough, and you need to fall back on some other techniques you've got stored up your sleeve.

I will throw another complicated title your way, as if all the emotional intelligence, psychological intelligence, and emotional agility weren't enough, and you are craving a bit more. We are going to be talking about:

Recognizing and channeling energies

Wow, quite something, conjuring up ideas of giant diggers ploughing through virgin land, or superpowers concentrating their strengths with laser-type precision.

It actually refers to emotions and the way we handle them. Think about a canal for a moment. There are waters, boats, and locks that the boats need to navigate. There are other features, for instance, most canals are pretty straight and run from one point to another.

So, apply that to emotion. We're in a state of panic (no news story, four hours and counting until the deadline). Let's bundle that panic, along with a few other emotions that accompany it, such as fear of failure, rejection, worry about the future, and peer pressure, among others.

We've got a bundle, and we put them in a canal boat—one of those long, thin vessels that chug along at walking speed but eventually get there. The canal is our road, the channel from where we were (panic plus the extras) to where we need to get to. That will likely be excitement, anticipated fulfillment, a sense of purpose, and an equal sense of camaraderie as we work things out together.

It's simple—all we need to do is get there. But it's not quite that simple. We must make the boat move from one place to another. Instead of fuel, we need techniques to move our boat along the canal to where we need it to be.

Consider an alternative scenario to illustrate the point. We have many disgruntled employees who are mad about an office closure or the necessary change to the bonus structure. Negotiations are fraught, and a solution looks impossible. What do we do?

We expand the seating on our canal boat and bundle all those employees on board. Then, we use special techniques to create a situation where we and others can manage the collective negative emotions and turn them into something quite different.

A conversation with employees close to the start of this canal journey might go something like this:

> You: *Hey, the countryside is beautiful and calming. You couldn't imagine it stuck in town.*

Employee: *Yeah, but what about our looming problems? Do you really want a strike?*

You: *Not at all; what I really need is to start with a blank piece of paper. Let's use these chalks and the roof of the canal boat.*

Employee: *What good is that going to do?*

You: *I thought we could start with one thing we both could freely give up. And don't come back with smoking, because I mean in terms of our positions on this situation. We both write something we can give up and then write something we must keep.*

Employee: *Well, I suppose it's worth a try.*

What we've done is take a step back, change the environment, and initiate a process of cooperation, both parties coming from a calmer place. We've reset the scene, almost like rebooting the computer when it gets clogged up beyond belief. You're enlarging the options for settlement, determined to get there before the journey is complete, but giving yourself time to look at all the possibilities. You're also removing the distractions and causes of enragement; you achieve this by separating the parties, yourself included, from the source of that enragement, the office closure or the letter that terminates the bonus scheme. You're also inviting the other party to help you develop a strategy toward a solution.

In other words, you're using your recently discovered emotional intelligence skills to turn a nasty negative into a resounding positive. You may have to compromise more than you expected, but that doesn't matter because you also utilize your skill set to build long-term relationships with your partners as the business advances. That gives you additional assets: trust, confidence, leadership, and teamwork.

So, what have we actually achieved? Well, look at it like this:

- We're not where we want to be.

- We need to get there, not just you but the whole team and all of those involved.

- What does jumping on board the canal boat actually do? Couldn't we get to our destination all the quicker by using the car? No? Really?

- The thing is that the journey is part of the process. The journey stills our natural tendencies; it can stop the panic trigger long before the squeeze begins. It separates us and rings-fences our problem while inviting possible solutions to visit.

- It's like rebooting your computer after you've cleaned it of all viruses. It gives you and others the time and space, free from distractions. It allows you to devise a plan that cultivates calm in the chaos all around.

CULTIVATING CALM IN MOMENTS OF CHAOS

Let's take an extreme example to make the point. You're a junior minister in a corrupt dictatorship where the masses of people are on the verge of a revolution. To paint you nicely, you've been increasingly worried about the direction of the government for some time.

Suddenly, it happens. The uprising starts. The presidential palace is besieged, the president is holed up in there, just like the thousands he's imprisoned through his ruthless determination not to lose power.

There is pure chaos everywhere. People are losing their lives, with soldiers firing on civilians and some soldiers turning on the presidential guard.

You feel a strong urge to take action. But what do you do?

First, given the rush and tears, you sit down and think. After a few minutes of meditation, it is vital to close off distractions and clear and calm the mind. Therefore, you ask for a paper and a pen.

"But people are losing their lives!" the exasperated guard commander says.

"I know," you reply, "but if we wade in without a plan, we'll cause more chaos. Chaos creates chaos; our first task is to replace it with calm and order. Call everyone you can find here to the ballroom, and we'll make a plan."

That gives you ten minutes to close your eyes, reflect, or meditate. You pause, breathe deeply, and feel a gradual grounding coming over you. If you manage it correctly, some very positive outcomes could result.

Reframe the situation.

What do you have to manage? There are rebels, the existing government headed by a desperate despot, and then you have the looters and the mass of ordinary people who just want to get on with their lives. You reflect that you have to manage expectations. Then, it comes to you—what you are really doing is managing emotions, yours inevitably, but a host of others, too.

You move on to dealing with those emotions, asking yourself what you are dealing with now. Right out front is fear and panic; close behind is anger. There are also milder emotions, such as disappointment, consternation, and apprehension. You must reframe these negative tendencies and transform them into positive goals, with the hope that they will yield positive outcomes.

Then, you know that you've hit on the right end of emotion:

> *Hope*
>
> *Hope, being one of the most positive emotions, pierces through the dark clouds of negative tendencies.*
>
> *Hope*

Returning to practical matters, with consideration of the triggers that lead to these negative tendencies. By understanding these, one can manage panic and fear and turn the situation into a hopeful one.

There's another aspect to all this that occurs to you just as a stream of worried faces joins you in the ballroom. The problem seems multi-faceted, but that's no bad thing on reflection. It might seem that any particular step could create new issues, but there is another way of looking at it: A multi-faceted situation can be broken down into its constituent parts. Thus, you have the problem of what to do with the old president, how to prevent the deaths, and how to stop the looters. Then, there's the long-hoped-for restoration of democracy.

Your thinking moves on at that point because surely the restoration of democracy is the ultimate aim.

"Take a seat on the floor, everyone. Good, is that everyone? Then I shall begin. We've got a chaotic scene being played out before us as I speak. Our objective is to turn the situation around to lay the foundations for the restoration of our democracy while ending the needless killing and looting. I don't know how we will achieve that, but I know where we need to be. You know, my second cousin, once removed, emigrated to America and started a factory. After a few years, the workers became angry with what the board was trying to do, believing they were being short-changed by the change process the business was undergoing. He told me how he packed everyone onto a canal boat, which slowed the whole anger thing. It gave them time to discuss, plan, and compromise. It gave them time to build for the future, and here today, we must never lose sight of the fact that we are building for the future."

Stirring words that were met with absolute silence, because you had managed through reflection and the emotional intelligence you had learned to bring everyone together with one aim, one plan for the future of your country.

You have taken panic and fear and replaced them with hope and aspiration, doing so through understanding and involving others.

In summary:

- Desperate situations call for desperate measures—right?

- Wrong—while sometimes desperate measures are needed (sinking ships and alien invasions come to mind), these trigger points need calm assessment before coming up with a plan.

- Just as chaos begets chaos, so calm breeds calmer. That means knowing yourself and understanding the reactions of those around you are excellent ways to turn a chaotic environment into a calm one.

CHAPTER SUMMARY: STAYING IN CONTROL

This chapter has been all about practical matters. It covers how we take the theories we've been investigating and turn them into steps to take in any situation. Whether you're a frantic news editor with nothing to write about and the deadline on your doorstep, the hassled factory owner who had a brilliant idea for a business but can't get everyone on the same side, or a worried government minister facing a revolution, you must face reality.

That reality is that you have a morass of negative tendencies, all triggered and firing off at each other, and somehow, you have to use your emotional intelligence to turn matters around. It does not matter whether it's a brilliant news story, the scoop of the year, a resolution to a long-running industrial dispute that threatened business, or the restoration of democracy in some country that is of vital importance to you, even if few people could find it on a map.

What matters is the techniques, knowledge, and experience you bring to the table. You used meditation to calm the panic. That meditation also recognized and understood the emotions at play and the triggers that set them off. You then used that understanding to craft a plan that would work, incorporating input from others to achieve the best possible situation.

That planning was inclusive, meaning you had the emotional intelligence to open the planning process up to others and benefit from their input. You also gained respect from others for the calm and courageous way you handled things.

Maybe, when those democratic elections come along, you might even put yourself up for the bigger job.

Handling crises effectively opens up the most significant opportunities.

SECOND PRINCIPLE
THE BUTTERFLY EFFECT

Employees essentially look up to their managers and mirror their behaviors. Therefore, when a manager is empathetic, it serves as an invitation for employees to apply the same empathy, which in turn benefits customers, the company, and the people they work with.

CHAPTER

LEADING BY EXAMPLE STARTS FROM WITHIN

"Be the change that you wish to see in the world."
— *Mahatma Gandhi, leader of the*
Indian Independence Movement

"Y"ou're going to the hospital in Scutari, mate, so good luck to yer."

"No, please, Sarge, not Scutari. I'll never get out alive."

The sergeant gave the soldier with the fractured leg a wink and moved on to the next broken body, noting his name as Private Endurance Hope, noting also how the red coats of the soldiers kept the blood from showing.

In the spring of 1855, he knew something that most people had yet to learn, and it gave him considerable hope. The arrival of Florence Nightingale the previous November had already transformed the hospital where she worked tirelessly. Sergeant Dove had a deep interest in repairing soldiers, believing the contract between government and individual extended beyond the point when the cannonball ripped into the body. He had gone to the hospital at every opportunity, inspired by Florence Nightingale's approach to nursing, which emphasized hygiene and professional care.

But what particularly impressed Sergeant Dove was the fact that she led from the front. She was no theoretical leader expounding ideas from some point of safety and comfort far from the fighting, but someone who showed how it should be done by getting involved and setting an example.

This story has a happy ending. Private Hope survived his injured leg, benefiting from the huge hygiene improvement at the Barrack Hospital in Scutari, such that within months of Nightingale's arrival, the death-by-infection rate had dropped from 42% to 2%. He led a long and colorful life, showing his scars to his children, grandchildren, and even the generation beyond that. Private Hope wasn't an educated man, far from it, but he always stressed the empathy that had impressed him so much with Florence Nightingale.

"She took the whole hospital with her," he would say, "infusing it with her ideal of saving lives through caring, understanding, and best practices in nursing."

Sergeant Dove stayed in the army, got a commission as an officer, and rose to brigadier. Never losing his interest in medicine, he came out of retirement to help establish the Royal Army Medical Corps in 1898, which is now the principal source of care for wounded soldiers. He, too, spoke of the way Florence Nightingale had led by determined example, bringing people along with her and leading them on to great things. He lived a long life, unaware that he had picked up the baton she had passed on to so many, developing and enhancing empathy to understand the emotions of others and adapting his care to accommodate their needs, even in a very often insensitive environment, such as the context of war.

Florence Nightingale is the third actor in our play, and the only real-life character of our trio. On coming home after the Crimean War, she set up the first ever school of nursing, and the profession never looked back. She inspired countless people to enter nursing and set the initial standards by which it was to be governed; some of those standards, such as professionalism, hygiene, and understanding the pain, fear, and hopes of those she treated, still endure today.

Miss Nightingale led by example. While there were nurses before her, she established nursing as a profession, one that has a purpose and can follow the principles embedded in empathy to this day. She was always on the ward, even at night, earning her the nickname "Lady with the Lamp." She carefully and patiently instructed her nurses on how to care, often showing them how to focus on the basics, such as hygiene, because that was what saved lives. She infused the hospitals she ran with a deep sense of caring and understanding of what the soldiers had been through. It's interesting to consider that a type of humanity could be found, even nearly 200 years ago, on the sad battlefield and in the hospitals behind the lines. Humanity arises from a simple understanding of what other people have gone through.

Whenever and wherever there is human interaction, there is the potential for empathy to flourish, and I hope for a day without soldiers and more peace, with more love and less war.

Ultimately, this is what Florence Nightingale taught those who followed her and the world at large. True humanity stems from compassion and allowing others to express and understand their feelings.

However, I want to bring another aspect to this story to your attention: she was also deeply reflective, and as a result, she knew herself very well, both in terms of her strengths and weaknesses. This is a vital aspect of leading by example. Being an inspiring leader, one who leads by example, requires self-awareness; in other words, you can develop self-awareness, play to your strengths, and address your weaknesses by acting as a role model.

There is also something far more significant: Only by knowing yourself can you truly understand others. By meeting your limitations, fears, and anxieties head-on, you can distinguish when they are about you and when they are about others. Everybody is different, so understanding what motivates and scares other people is a crucial aspect of leadership.

It's called empathy, something Florence Nightingale was familiar with and utilized to her advantage.

The fictional Sergeant Dove is an excellent example of someone inspired by leadership, but it also illustrates another benefit of this inspirational style. I gave him the name because doves are associated with healing, which I wanted to highlight.

The sergeant had misgivings about the appalling medical care experienced by wounded soldiers, feeling instinctively that it was wrong to leave them wallowing in pain and filth. Yet, he did not know what to do about it until Florence Nightingale arrived in Crimea and began making the significant changes she implemented. Her leadership focused on his sense of purpose, and both ended up adding volumes to medical care on and after the terrible event, which involved a battlefield.

The benefit comes from the contagious nature, and I'm not talking about the nasty spreadable disease that Florence Nightingale worked so hard to eliminate from her hospitals.

This was a positive contagion involving inspiration, motivation, determination, and focus. It all started with one woman and grew from there, with generations of inspired people adding to the movement. Sergeant Dove was just one of millions over time.

Florence Nightingale wasn't a saint. She could be crabby and difficult, not always tolerant, and so driven by ambition to the extent that she turned down several offers of marriage. That placed a strain on her character, already susceptible to fits of depression. Incidentally, she also suffered from exhaustion, which was hardly surprising. The point is that she was aware of her weaknesses and strengths in the areas of organization, ceaseless care, and discipline. She used this awareness to her advantage, making her one of the most obvious historical examples of someone who led by example, charging ahead from the front.

This story exemplifies the concept of leading by example. It purposefully contextualizes it in an environment where empathy is often lacking, demonstrating that compassion, kindness, and leading by example can be applied in any context.

CHAPTER SUMMARY: LEADING BY EXAMPLE

This chapter illustrates that leading by example is the very essence of effective leadership. It allows you to inspire others to lead in the same way.

Empathic leaders tend to lead by example naturally, as they understand the feelings, concerns, and hopes of others, and set a model to overcome them.

The capacity to influence others is a powerful force; when coupled with empathy, leading by example flows down from the initial leader and inspires others to lead in an emotionally intelligent way, triggering a chain reaction of benefits that lead to further benefits.

Self-awareness is the foundation you should focus on to efficiently lead by example. By understanding your strengths and weaknesses, you can recognize, improve, and utilize the strengths and weaknesses of those working for you.

PART 4
EMPATHY

THIRD PRINCIPLE
THE VIRTUOUS CIRCLE

Employees are consciously or unconsciously aligning themselves for the benefit or detriment of their managers, and for this reason, managers should apply empathy and care to benefit from positive attraction.

CHAPTER

8

BECOMING AN
EMPATHIC LEADER

> *"Empathy is a choice. It's a vulnerable choice because in order to connect with you, I have to connect with something in myself that knows that feeling."*
> — Brené Brown, U.S. author and researcher

DEFINITION

Empathy brings everything into play. Empathy spearheads emotional intelligence. It's inclusive, multiplying any individual's efforts many times over. It is a harness that brings all into the fold, so they might contribute their ideas, talent, and hard work to the output. More than that, it encourages contributions and builds confidence, so the shy, bright person who never used to contribute speaks up and shares their thoughts. And empathy grows as success happens. There can't be a better example of success breeding success.

When all is said and done, empathy will forge a way forward because it involves you, as the leader, combining the best contributions from each team member, encouraging them to share their ideas, and outlining what they can do to bring the solution to the problem into reality.

So, what is empathy, this wonderful drug, this cure for all evils?

Empathy, in simple terms, is the ability to understand what someone else is going through and share the same feeling with them, thereby being compassionate. By putting yourself in their shoes, walking that mile, you build an understanding of what they are thinking and feeling. There are two angles to empathy:

- Cognitive empathy gives one the ability to see things from that person's perspective, as if looking through that person's eyes.

- While emotional empathy is just as it sounds—you can feel what they are feeling.

Of course, it is possible to have both types of empathy, allowing you to feel with the other person and see the world through their eyes.

Whichever type of empathy you develop first, it gives you the ability to produce a feeling of compassion and a connected response.

We've looked at leaders like Florence Nightingale, who led by example, creating a powerful movement for better nursing that improved the world as a whole. I want to bring in another leader, this one firmly from the 20th century, and one person will remember clearly.

Mother Teresa was born in Macedonia in 1910. This woman, now Saint Teresa of Calcutta, possessed an extraordinary amount of empathy when she died eighty-seven years later, probably enough to fill a football stadium. Many people are unaware that she had a remarkable upbringing in Macedonia, where her mother instilled in her a deep empathy.

Furthermore, the empathy she displayed throughout her long life was multiplied many times over due to its contagious nature. Put bluntly, when adequately exercised, empathy can spread like wildfire, producing returns after returns on the original investment of time, understanding, and kindness.

This concept is embodied in most religions and the minds of many non-believers. It is believed that empathy fosters empathy, contributing to a better world.

It is also a principle of the *Emotional Intelligence Theory* encapsulated by the *Butterfly Effect*.

Of course, there are arguments in favor of the opposite, arguments that many dictators throughout history would have been all too familiar with.

> *Empathy is a weakness; it can go overboard with kindness.*
>
> *Who is in charge here? Someone needs to be decisive and even ruthless.*

These arguments stand because they contain some elements of truth. Let's look at a couple of examples:

Empathy is weakness. The argument goes that being overly kind is oddly compatible with corporate objectives because it allows for too much flexibility when a firm response is required.

The response is that empathy requires courage to implement because it involves sharing your plans and ideas with the entire team. The purpose of this is to gain everyone's cooperation, enabling you to meet corporate objectives sooner and more efficiently. It takes much courage to manage in an empathetic manner because you are exposing yourself. Ultimately, empathy becomes a strength due to its contagious nature and the receiver's desire to reciprocate.

Who is in charge here? Someone needs to be decisive and even ruthless. This argument goes that business is not a democracy, and rule by committee will always be the poor cousin to decisive leadership.

The answer to that point of view is, yes, I see your point (after all, I am an empathetic leader), but you are looking at it the wrong way around. Being decisive is often essential in business, but being open-minded is equally important. Remember, taking everyone on that boat is critical. It would be a terrible shame to run a business into the ground on an *'I'm being decisive'* trip, while ignoring the views of people who may even have more experience than you.

Being decisive is essential in business, but it is often mistaken for being impulsive and dictatorial. It's far better to reach out to gather all views, encourage others to speak up, even when they disagree with you, consider everything, and then think about all the options. When you've done that, by all means, turn around and do your *'I'm being decisive'* bit. As the leader, you're responsible for making the final decision anyway, and no one will take it out of your hands; you're being paid for it. Still, only an exceedingly silly person or an inexperienced leader ignores opposing points of view before settling on a course of action.

Empathy is a powerful asset in business. More than any other component of a company, it is the glue that holds things together while also keeping them far enough apart that each individual can contribute in a way that maximizes their skills and experience.

It is even more powerful because it is such a rare trait in today's leaders. Consequently, it presents a fantastic opportunity to set yourself apart and allow the power of attraction to work in your favor.

People often discuss property, capital, and labor as the three key components of a business. There should be a fourth, and—you've guessed it—that would be empathy.

Summary

- Cognitive Empathy is understanding someone else's perspective, and emotional empathy is the capacity to feel what someone else is feeling. Both are powerful and should be developed as part of your emotional intelligence capability.

- Empathy has many positive associations, including encouraging more of itself.

- Empathy carries even more positive meaning in challenging times.

- Inevitably, there are arguments against, and these tend to rest on empathy being too inclusive, resulting in a gap in authority, which we will delve into in the next chapter, with the concept of *Parameter of Healthy Empathy*.

- For the moment, what we should keep in mind is that an empathetic approach requires more courage and decisiveness than a dictatorial alternative, and the long-term benefits outweigh the short-term 'loss of authority.'

EMPATHIC LEADERSHIP DEVELOPS CHARISMA

Empathy is a key component of a business that consistently gives back. Properties become contaminated or overbuilt, storms rage through, and assets become exhausted. Capital is squandered, misappropriated, or distributed in the form of dividends to boost the share price. Labor grows old and retires or moves on to other endeavors, sometimes after a significant investment in training, which can be intensely frustrating.

Empathy, however, stays the course. A good leader who manages according to the principles of the *Emotional Intelligence Theory* will recognize the benefits, including attracting positivity, increasing people's engagement, and becoming an inspiration, which inevitably leads to their own success and the success of those around them.

The benefits of the *Emotional Intelligence Theory* continue to flourish, with a single, straightforward cause. People can easily recognize an empathetic leader and want to follow them because that empathy inspires them. There's a gravitational pull that works sideways, up, down, and inside out.

People love the idea of being consulted frequently, to be listened to, cared for, and recognized.

What does that mean in practical terms? It means that when the empathetic marketing manager places a job vacancy advertisement, marketing receives many more applicants than production, which operates on a more traditional management style. There is a force of attraction and underlying benefits of empathy that are greater than what some may perceive as a weakness. Marketing gets the pick of the crop, further underlining the strength of the department.

They also get fewer leavers. While sometimes, a manager may want someone to leave (that in itself can be a product of a lack of empathy), more often a departure represents a waste of valuable training resources, a gap before a replacement is found, followed by another bout of recruitment and training efforts, and a noticeable moral impact on the team.

The empathetic manager is, by nature, closer to people and, for this reason, more charismatic, even if this is not an initial intent, because being empathetic is genuine and egoless. Still, it's a fragile condition, of course. Similarly, empathy is not always natural and easy to apply. However, it should be practiced and cultivated as often as possible.

People instinctively follow successful leaders.

Back in the day, leading often involved going into battle at the head of your troops, which might have been the way to do things. Nowadays, there's another option: opening up to ideas and possible solutions and then deciding as a leader while taking everyone with you.

Sadly, empathy is often the most neglected aspect of business success. That's often because people mistakenly think it opens the way for rules by committee, which, as we've seen, most definitely does not. It is a misconception, and it is undoubtedly a proven lack of practice. Other leaders believe they don't have the time, which is a short-term perspective, because the time spent now will save you much time later.

A third category of empathy deniers is those who don't want to undertake the foundational work of emotional intelligence, specifically self-awareness and self-regulation.

They either don't want to get to know themselves, believe they already do, or avoid learning to self-regulate—often under the false assumption that they can already manage themselves just fine, or that it's unnecessary.

This phenomenon of denial or ignorance about emotional intelligence in business has a surprising kick-back, an almost ironic sting in the tail.

Leaders who operate by following the principles inherent in an empathetic approach are often admired and even revered, precisely because it remains a rare trait in today's leaders' personality.

Satya Nadella, Microsoft's CEO, is a good example of someone broadly recognized for this rare capacity. When he took the top job, he was determined to put relationships at the center. He encouraged a mindful approach at every level of the business to bring out the best in every employee, allowing them to contribute significantly—and sometimes in surprising ways—to the company's future success.

In short, he changed Microsoft beyond recognition. What has that done for the business? Not only has it led to a new lease on life with significantly increased involvement and empowerment, but it has also made Microsoft a magnet for talent. Not only that, but Microsoft's revenue and profit have grown significantly since Mr. Nadella took on his role, which is further proof that applying the concept of emotional intelligence does not weaken leadership and business.

People follow success, and the *Emotional Intelligence Theory* is purposely founded on principles that think 'people first,' encouraging you to get the best out of them and be recognized for it.

That means we have a situation where empathy and charisma are often closely aligned.

In simple words:

- Empathy is a self-regenerating resource available to business leaders that both keeps on giving and stays the course.

- Empathic leaders naturally draw people in like a magnet, giving themselves a competitive advantage in today's marketplace, where people precisely want to work for empathetic leaders.

CHAPTER SUMMARY:
DEVELOPING AN EMPATHIC LEADERSHIP STYLE

We started this chapter asking ourselves what empathy is. We defined it as the ability to understand other people's emotions and feelings and to react accordingly—at least, that's the shorthand version.

We discussed two types of empathy: (1) cognitive (understanding situations from someone's perspective), and (2) emotional empathy (where we can feel what someone is feeling). People can develop either of these, or both.

Then, we studied Mother Teresa as a shining example of a lifelong commitment to empathy; although she may not have recognized it as such, she effectively applied the *Emotional Intelligence Theory* by leading with an empathetic style. It is also essential to realize that numerous other examples can be found in all religions.

Next, we discussed the fact that not everyone adopts the empathetic approach to business leadership. There are three broad types of deniers. These are (1) based on perceptions of it leading to weak leadership, (2) not having the time to delve into it, and (3) not wanting to get involved in the process of developing themselves toward more emotional intelligence.

Then, we went into a couple of unique and fascinating concepts. The first concerns the charismatic draw of empathetic leaders—how everyone wants to work for them and how this keeps giving back because empathy is like a tree that grows and flourishes unless something comes along, threatening to chop it down.

9

WITHIN THE PARAMETER OF HEALTHY EMPATHY

"Do not confuse gentle with weak, or kindness with naïve.
Strong people can be soft. Wise people can be kind."
— L.R. Knost, U.S. author and social justice advocate

So, we delved into understanding empathy. I can see some clear benefits, and I have gone through the process of getting to know myself and regulating my behavior.

What do I do now? Do I charge ahead and 'listen' to everyone's conflicting emotions? A danger here is best illustrated by a sales director whom I once knew in a company, early in my career.

Pete was about as friendly and empathetic as you could get. Whether he had undergone a training program or it came naturally, I don't know.

There's a very good reason why I don't know: Shortly after being made the chief executive of a subsidiary company, he was reorganized and disappeared. I've often reflected on this and once asked my boss about his vanishing act.

The answer I got is worth repeating:

> *Pete was nice enough, certainly. He could see anybody else's point of view and tried very hard to accommodate their differing slants on the problems of the day.*
>
> *And that was his downfall. He was unable to pick a path through everybody's emotions that was guided by anything.*
>
> *I don't want to make an analogy of a sailing ship buffeted this way and that in a storm, but it was a bit like that.*

When I asked how else it could be done, the answer my boss gave astounded me:

> *You need to establish your management style within a firm framework of principles. I sometimes think that with Pete, if someone had sincerely told him that the way to meet the sales targets that quarter was to give it all away, he would have gone down that route.*
>
> *You need to fit the way you lead into the values you hold dear.*

Well, that blew my mind, and I've often thought about it.

My boss at the time was hardly the most empathetic creature on earth. In fact, we used to call him by the nickname of a famous, ruthless Mongol leader.

But, from that day forth, I refrained from mentioning Genghis Khan. Instead, I thought long and hard about the pearls that Genghis... sorry, my boss, contributed to my development of ideas on business leadership.

DEFINITION

To be healthy, empathy requires a framework within which to operate safely, or you become 'too kind,' or naïve, to put it bluntly. In that, the naysayers we referred to in the previous chapter are not entirely wrong. Empathy cannot be offered to anyone at any time or in any way.

In fact, the framework should be fairly rigid to ensure empathy is applied healthily and avoid people taking advantage of you.

The fences should be built around key values, with their intersection forming the parameters of healthy empathy.

Those values are your *personal values*, your company's values, also called *corporate values*, and common sense, which we will refer to as *universal values*. Although there are always nuances to common sense based on cultural context, for example, most common sense remains... well, common.

This leads naturally to a Venn diagram, to help you visualize the parameters of healthy empathy, within which empathy can be practiced freely and as often as possible:

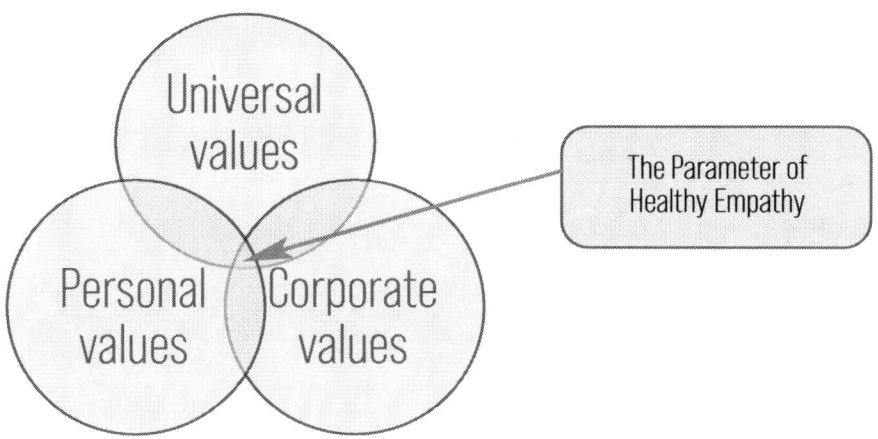

THE SWEET SPOT

This is where it gets exciting because, with some values surrounding the empathetic approach, you don't blow in the direction the last breath of wind sends you. You stay true to a course and use those values to guide the ship to its destination.

But there is more, because, within this "sweet spot," empathy can be used safely, not something your average authoritarian leader will want you to believe.

Universal Values

The most obvious framework from which to operate is *fairness*. A value for which people have been fighting forever, regardless of their origins, culture, or religion. Thus, this value is universal.

Another significant value for most humans is *trust*, with a generous degree of *autonomy*. Hence, you might want everyone on the team to have their say before you make a decision, because you trust them to provide valuable insight and think that they'll feel part of the decision, which, ultimately, they will have responsibility for delivering.

Consideration, also referred to as being valued, is sometimes misinterpreted as being rewarded, but it is another vital value for those who work for you. Now, most people think of rewards as financial or a pat on the back, leaving you with the slight hope that there may be some dollars in your pocket the next time you shine.

However, consideration can encompass a wide range of things, including recognition, praise, extra responsibility, promotion, project leadership, or additional training in a field that you and your employees believe will benefit them.

Perhaps the easiest reward you can give those working for you is an empathetic culture, where everyone feels respected. Thus, it is natural to list *respect* and *leading by example* as universal values.

Many people say they go to work for the money (which is true in most cases), but they also show up and offer their contributions because they feel valued and respected, and they want to continue giving to a management style that gives generously, leading by example. This means there is a drive toward following people who lead by using emotional intelligence.

Personal Values

By definition, Personal Values will differ by... yes, by person! What one human being holds to be important may not feature on the list of another. That does not mean it isn't essential; it simply means it's not universally shared.

Inevitably, there are standard features that make some personal values almost universal–almost, but not quite. Take punctuality for instance. Many people believe this is a key value for those in the workplace. Yet there are those for whom punctuality is not so much of a big deal, particularly if you consider that some of your employees may stay up all night working on a project with brilliant results, only to get to the progress meeting, late by 5 minutes the following morning.

Personal values encompass both common and uncommon values that individuals hold, often unique to the leader you are, reminding us that the world is diverse and complex. And thank goodness that it is.

Corporate Values

Now, we move to the third category: Corporate Values.

"But," you might say, "surely a company is just a group of people because any business is just the people that work in it?"

Yes, that's correct, but it doesn't mean that the founders and/or current company leaders cannot and will not have values they want you to apply to the company as it conducts its day-to-day business. A good example is excellent customer service. This might have sub-values or targets, such as responding to customers' emails within a day or answering the phone promptly. Outstanding customer service is not a universal value because it does not apply to all business operations in the same way that fairness or respect for all do. It may be less important to some companies than to others, often depending on the company's industry.

Corporate values are chosen and form part of the corporation's character. As such, as with personal values, they can be familiar or obscure.

Another example of corporate value could be prompt payment to suppliers (I admit it may not be very inspiring, but for the sake of this example, it should work just fine). This becomes fascinating because some would argue that this is a key aspect of fairness; however, to understand corporate values completely, you need to step back from a moral position and recognize that, other than actual universal values, there is no moral position within the corporate world. A company can validly define itself as an entity that pays as late as possible, while others might see benefit in paying immediately.

CHAPTER SUMMARY: WITHIN
THE PARAMETER OF HEALTHY EMPATHY

In this chapter, we discovered that to avoid being naïve or senselessly kind, applying healthy empathy requires defined parameters, constituting a "sweet spot" where personal, corporate, and universal values intersect (the intersection of the Venn diagram).

Interestingly, empathy and compassion can be applied freely and safely within this space, without worrying about being too kind; in fact, they can and should be used as often as possible.

CHAPTER

10

THE RECIPROCITY PRINCIPLE: WHAT YOU GIVE IS WHAT YOU GET

> *"When a human is guided by the principles of reciprocity*
> *and consciousness, they are not far from the moral law.*
> *Whatever you don't wish for yourself, don't do unto others."*
> *(adapted for inclusive language)*
> *Confucius – Chinese Philosopher*

HOW EMPATHY BUILDS TRUST AND LOYALTY

The reciprocity principle reminds me of a religious figure who became a good friend. He had no connection to business and, despite being highly intelligent, wouldn't have the slightest idea what a balance sheet was; he probably associated it with lying on his bed sheets at night and balancing the day with his maker.

So, his contribution to my business understanding was zero.

Or was it? You see, he taught me one lesson in particular that has stayed with me. At first, I thought his words were a joke, but after seeing a few examples, I realized their seriousness.

Every time he gave away what others might hang on to, something came back to him. As I progressed through business leadership, I realized that there was something valuable for the corporate world.

Giving and receiving are interchangeable in the sense that when you give to others, you receive it back either immediately or later on. But you do receive, and there's a good reason for this.

You're building trust.

Think of trust in construction terms. You pour it into the foundations, and the building lasts forever, or as long as you can maintain that trust. You put it into your design thinking, and it repays you with superb visuals and excellent efficiency.

So, it is with a team.

Trust is naturally created from every act of kindness, compassion, and empathy, which in turn strengthens the team.

And because they all get their turn at creating, trust creates loyalty.

So, let's ask ourselves what loyalty is:

1.   It's both an emotional and behavioral commitment.

2.   It has a profoundly positive impact.

3.   It serves as a powerful motivator.

4.   It's a multiplier—loyalty inspires more loyalty.

In essence, empathy forms a chain of positive reactions, which not only benefits the leader, given that '*employees are consciously or unconsciously aligning themselves for the benefit or detriment of their managers'* (Principle 3: The Virtuous Circle), but also has a contagious effect, because *'employees essentially look up to their managers and mirror their behavior. Therefore, when a manager is empathetic, it serves as an invitation for employees to apply the same empathy, which in turn benefits customers, the company, and the people they work with'* (Principle 2: The Butterfly Effect).

EMPATHY: YOUR COMPETITIVE ADVANTAGE

Sadly, just like the saying that 'common sense ain't so common,' empathy is not that prevalent in the world of work today. However, it is a trend that will continue... well, trending.

There has always been considerable friction in the workplace. Several decades ago, workers were there just to run the machines or dig the coal for endless hours until they either got maimed or died from disease or exhaustion.

At which point, there would always be another worker to fill that place.

Thankfully, the world has moved on from there—COVID-19 and the digitalization of the world have completely rebalanced the strength in favor of the workforce, which now has the luxury of choosing what to get involved with and what not to.

At the beginning, as humans emerged, the primary 'job' was to obtain food and shelter. Slowly, through the accumulation of reserves and the organizational aspects of a tribal race, other occupations branched out from there. We got warriors, artists, traders, and leaders.

Skip forward a few hundred years, and we have thousands of occupations. Scratch that, we must have hundreds of thousands. Moreover, the Gen Z and Millennial generations, in particular, possess the skills and adaptability to transition between various jobs and occupations. Gone are the days when you did an apprenticeship in drafting and stayed with the same firm until retirement, by which time you had become a drawing office manager.

The modern world is all about choice. We have a choice over what we spend our money on and, even more importantly, we have a choice over how we earn that money.

This means leaders today need to recognize that they don't have a captive workforce and that the world has moved on. Moreover, it continues to move on, with or without them.

Accepting this is one thing.

Embracing it through the understanding and application of the *Emotional Intelligence Theory* is another.

Take a simple example. Twenty years ago, people went to work. Now, very often work comes to them. People work from home, and the trend is growing and becoming increasingly the norm, particularly among younger generations who have grown up and matured with the technology that makes it possible.

As a leader, you can either resist this or embrace it.

As long as you apply emotional intelligence, you can take a whole new generation of people with you, who are ready to commit, but not at any price anymore.

LIVING THE LONG GAME OF EXCEPTIONAL LEADERSHIP

"Well, all I can say is I tried this empathetic stuff, and it got me nowhere fast."

"Oh, that's surprising. Can you tell me more about what you did?"

"Sure, I had a meeting this morning and asked everyone to give their point of view."

"So, let me get this right, you adopted this new leadership style and gave it this morning to get results."

"Yeah, I mean I got results, sure enough, but not what I expected at all. Some of my people started sharing their opinions, which opened Pandora's boxes of issues, which they described as never settled."

"Yes, I think I see the problem. Let me explain again how this works. You see…"

The first thing I needed to convey was that the empathetic leadership style encourages a new dynamic—a way of thinking that is honest and transparent, based on trust, respect, and care.

Trust, respect, and care are essential parts of building relationships, and trust isn't like shaking your pepper dispenser to color your plate. It takes time.

That means you carry on. You ride out the skeptics and prove the naysayers wrong. You build trust patiently, demonstrating care and understanding.

A long time ago, I observed someone being appointed as a department manager in the finance department. This particular department had two traits I noted at the time:

1. It clashed with every other department in the business over nearly every aspect of its operations.

2. Ditto for within the department—for instance, credit control squabbled endlessly with management accounts or the general ledger clerk.

This was an education for me because the person involved in management had no management experience, other than training in the armed forces, where compassion and empathy weren't highly emphasized.

This manager was replaced, and the new one opened my eyes because, from her first day in the job, she approached things in a way that was different from anything I had experienced before. She included people, asking for their opinions before making a decision.

This gave her a reputation for being indecisive. I expected her to buckle at that, but far from it; she remained firm and consistent. As her decisions proved correct, the jokes about her dropped away, and she gained respect amongst senior leaders.

But also among her staff. Not only for her sound decision-making, but also because she treated those who worked with her fairly and with respect.

It took a couple of years, but by the time she got promoted to a divisional role (and presumably started all over again), she had stopped the squabbles. She produced a department that was a driving force within the business, respected by other functions, so that when they took a stance, other managers and line employees accepted the sense in her position.

Emotional intelligence is all about the long term, building trust and respect steadily, recognizing that these qualities are reciprocal, and that empathy will continue to grow, even after the original instigators have moved on.

This chapter, in many ways, represents the core of the *Emotional Intelligence Theory*.

CHAPTER SUMMARY:
EMBRACING THE BENEFITS OF EMPATHY

By now, it is clear that empathy carries a wealth of benefits in human interactions. In this chapter, we discovered that giving and receiving are incredibly connected. As we extend empathy and care for others, we also receive back, either immediately or later on. We may receive tangible benefits or, through an extension of cooperation, namely trust, respect, and, further down the line, loyalty, which are essential components of healthy human relationships.

People, especially nowadays, with so many choices available, gravitate toward either empathetic leaders or, sadly, dictatorial ones.

The benefits of empathy accumulate over time and spread contagiously, inspiring more of itself and a whole new generation of people determined to contribute in brand-new ways, giving the empathetic leader a competitive advantage.

Well done, the foundation of emotional intelligence is now laid out, and you can build on it the next layer, which will focus on adaptability, a critical aspect of applying emotional intelligence and managing people interactions efficiently.

PART 5
PSYCHOLOGICAL INTELLIGENCE

FOURTH PRINCIPLE
UNDERSTANDING OTHERS AND
ADAPTING YOUR EMOTIONS

*Using emotional agility to deal with others is essential
in people management; therefore, a manager must
develop psychological intelligence to read personalities and
emotions effectively, to best respond to them.*

CHAPTER

11

BECOMING PSYCHOLOGICALLY INTELLIGENT

"The sign of an intelligent people is their ability to control their emotions by the application of reason."
— *Marya Mannes, U.S. writer and author of* The Fashionable Mind *(1960)*

DEFINITION

L et's start this section with a reminder as to what psychological intelligence is. Back in Chapter 2, we defined it as the *ability to understand how people react and behave in particular circumstances.*

Another way to look at it is that you can decipher others' personalities and the emotions involved in situations.

Both are correct, as they approach the definition from slightly different perspectives. Whether we talk about people's reactions to events or their personalities in various situations, it amounts to much the same thing.

We're dealing with the interaction between you (the one who claims possession of psychological intelligence) and those around you.

So, why is psychological intelligence so critical to the application of emotional intelligence? The answer is that there's a word in each definition of vital importance. In the first, it's 'understand,' in the second, it's 'decipher.' They are both verbs and involve Eureka moments, when one suddenly sees the light, or realizes and recognizes the significance.

READING SITUATIONS

It's time to leave theory and definitions behind us and return to the practical world. If, in any given situation, you are aware of the attitude of another party present, you have a definitive edge. Indeed, that edge can be decisive in handling confrontations or negotiations.

In the 18th century, duels between gentlemen were relatively common, making them a suitable setting for TV and movies today. They often fought for honor, at least in fiction; maybe in reality, there was more greed involved.

You wake up tomorrow, not in bed, but transported back three hundred years. Trying to work out what has happened, you're careless and, before you know it, you've been challenged to a duel. A second appears from nowhere, and the next morning, you're standing in a misty field at dawn, staring at the prospect of oblivion.

Now, time travel hasn't yet been mastered, so this needs a fair bit of imagination, but what if you knew this person well enough to comprehend what he was feeling as he stared at the oblivion you might send his way?

You know your feelings; fear and apprehension must be near the top of the stack. You appreciate that this might affect your aim, so tell yourself to stay calm and take your time as you face one of the best shots in the land.

Someone with psychological intelligence, however, can take this one step further. They know their own emotions but can also read and decipher those of their "opponent." Perhaps they realize that this cool cucumber aiming right now is actually madly in love and the last person on earth willing to forfeit their life. You make a split-second decision, and rather than waiting to let off your pistol, you fire it deliberately way above his head. He levels his sights on you, squeezes the trigger, and then jerks his pistol up into the air. Honor is satisfied, and no blood is spilt. You go your separate ways, but meet up by accident later and, somehow, you're out on the town together, or whatever the term was back in the 18th century.

Later that night, you get whizzed back to the present, and you breathe a sigh of relief to be back in modern times when a bullet in your chest is treatable, and you have a better than even chance of coming out in one piece.

Inevitably, you reflect on your experience, wanting to know more about yourself and following the best traditions you've developed of self-knowledge, leading to self-awareness. Your first shout is that you had much courage to fire over your opponent's head deliberately, knowing that leeches would likely bleed you if you'd been shot that day.

But your second thought is that, while courage played a part, your psychological intelligence won out for you.

Your psychological intelligence enabled you to recognize the emotions he felt and build upon that by understanding what those emotions would lead him to do.

Proving that psychological intelligence can save your bacon while enhancing your experience and gaining the respect of those who oppose you.

CHAPTER SUMMARY:
BECOMING PSYCHOLOGICALLY INTELLIGENT

Marya Mannes's quote at the start of this chapter connects intelligence with the ability to manage or control one's emotions. Psychological intelligence is just that, but with others.

We reviewed the definition of psychological intelligence, noting that it starts with understanding or deciphering the emotions others are experiencing. This is a critical component of applying the *Emotional Intelligence Theory*, which consists of benefiting from a thorough understanding of people's emotions and how they typically respond.

In essence, we've a situation where we are examining a vital concept of emotional intelligence, which enables us to decipher people and situations, to anticipate and understand their reactions.

To make the point of the usefulness of psychological intelligence, we looked at a simple case study—the duel—in which one protagonist, who happened also to be a time traveler, looked back on his duel with the realization that, yes, he had exhibited bravery, but the key aspect that led to his survival had been his capacity to read the situation and what he could do with that courage. He knew how to handle the situation because he was psychologically intelligent—that ability we can develop to decipher and understand others and anticipate their actions.

CHAPTER

12

HOW TO READ PEOPLE

"Eyes are more accurate witnesses than ears."
— Heraclitus, ancient Greek philosopher

UNCOVERING DIFFERENT
PERSONALITIES AND MINDSETS

It's time to baffle the mind with lots of clever-sounding initials to categorize personality type, taken from the Myers-Briggs daughter-and-mother combination, who put together the Myers-Briggs Type Indicator (MBTI) in the mid-20th century, focusing on four cognitive dimensions (Introversion/Extraversion, Sensing/Intuition, Thinking/Feeling, Judging/Perceiving). However, popular modern personality sites, such as 16Personalities, later added user-friendly names for a broader range of personality types, for clarity's sake. It is also probably important to highlight again that there is no affiliation, and the study that follows is based on publicly available personality typology theory inspired by the MBTI.

Let's take a look at the different personality types, but this time from a perspective that goes beyond self-awareness, to the standpoint of psychological intelligence, or understanding others.

For each personality type, you will be presented with the MBTI format (4 letters), the personality name (as per the 16Personalities website), the personality's primary emotions immediately below, and then, the recommended way to interact with them in bullet points.

It is also important to reiterate that there is no affiliation, and the study that follows is based on publicly available personality typology theory, inspired by the MBTI®, a registered trademark of the Myers & Briggs Foundation, used here for educational and illustrative purposes.

ANALYSTS – Intuitive and Thinking

INTJ – The Architect

Reserved, Imaginative, Independent, Highly analytical, and Quiet emotions.

- Respect their need for alone time to process emotions.

- Approach with logical, strategic discussions.

- Avoid forcing emotional sharing; build trust gradually.

- Appreciate their vision and independence.

INTP – The Logician

Curious, Calm, Inventive, Intellectual, and Confused when overwhelmed

- Engage in intellectual discussions.

- Give them space to think and analyze.

- Avoid emotional pressure or small talk.

- Appreciate their originality and insight.

ENTJ – The Commander

Bold, Confident, Determination, Decisive, and Frustrated when blocked

- Be direct and goal-focused.

- Respect their leadership and vision.

- Avoid inefficiency or indecisiveness.

Appreciate their strategic thinking.

ENTP – The Debater

Energetic, Optimist, Outspoken, Quick Thinker, and Close at sharing deep emotions

- Engage in lively debates and idea exchanges.

- Be open to new perspectives.

- Avoid overly rigid or controlling behavior.

- Appreciate their quick wit and inventiveness.

DIPLOMATS – Intuitive and Feeling

INFJ – The Advocate

Insightful, Empathetic, Future-oriented, and Stressed from others' emotions

Engage in meaningful, deep conversations.

Be patient and avoid rushing them.

Respect their need for privacy and reflection.

Support their idealistic and empathetic nature.

INFP – The Mediator

Sensitive, Hopeful, Altruistic, Harmonious, Authentic, and Do not trust easily

Be supportive and validate their feelings.

Encourage their ideals and creativity.

Avoid harsh criticism or dismissiveness.

Give them space and time to reflect, express values, and trust you in return.

ENFJ – The Protagonist

Charismatic, Inspiring, Empathetic, Cooperative, and Stress from discord

Engage in meaningful, heartfelt conversations.

Be supportive and sincere.

Avoid superficiality or dismissiveness.

Respect their need for harmony and connection.

ENFP – The Campaigner

Optimist, Enthusiastic, Imaginative, Sociable, and Emotionally sensitive

Be open and enthusiastic.

Encourage their creativity and ideas.

Be sensitive to their emotional highs and lows.

Support their need for meaningful connections.

SENTINELS – Sensing and Judging

ISTJ – The Logistician

Practical, Responsible, Detail-focused, Structured, and Anxious without plans

- Be organized and logical; avoid emotional arguments.
- Respect their need for structure and predictability.
- Give them space to process emotions privately.
- Acknowledge their sense of duty and reliability.

ISFJ – The Defender

Organized, Detail-oriented, Empathetic, Loyal, and Anxious if unappreciated

- Show appreciation and recognize their contributions.
- Be gentle and avoid harsh criticism.
- Respect their desire to help and protect others.
- Provide reassurance to ease their anxieties.

ESTJ – The Executive

Organized, Assertive, Efficient, Optimist, and may come across as Insensitive

- Be efficient and organized.
- Respect their leadership and decisiveness.
- Avoid wasting time or being disorganized.
- Appreciate their drive for results.

ESFJ – The Consul

Friendly, Caring, Socially warm, Cooperative, and Anxious about harmony

- Be warm and cooperative.

- Show appreciation and respect for social norms.

- Avoid conflict and be diplomatic.

- Support their desire to help and connect.

EXPLORERS – Sensing and Perceiving

ISTP – The Virtuoso

Bold, Practical, Hands-on, Curious, Problem-solver, and Emotional detachment

- Give them freedom to explore and experiment.

- Be straightforward and practical.

- Avoid micromanaging or emotional appeals.

- Appreciate their hands-on problem-solving skills.

ISFP – The Adventurer

Artistic, Sensitive, Spontaneous, and Intense emotional expressiveness

- Be gentle and nonjudgmental.

- Respect their need for personal freedom and expression.

- Encourage their creativity and spontaneity.

- Avoid pushing them into rigid plans.

ESTP – The Entrepreneur

Energetic, Perceptive, Spontaneity, Action-oriented, and Lack of sensitivity

- Be direct and action-oriented.

- Provide opportunities for hands-on experiences.

- Avoid rigid routines or excessive detail.

- Match their energy and enthusiasm.

ESFP – The Entertainer

Outgoing, Fun-loving, Enthusiastic, Sensitive, and Impulsive

- Be lively and engaging.

- Appreciate their sociability and warmth.

- Avoid negativity or criticism in public.

- Encourage their spontaneity and fun-loving nature.

'But...' you may think, '...why even care about the four letters describing each personality type? Aren't the related names more friendly and easier to remember anyway?'

Well, yes, but allow me to remind you that what interests you here is becoming familiar with how to read people, and the four letters will help us to do just that: decoding personalities.

Let's play a game. I want you to think about someone you know very well, and someone you meet often but don't necessarily know intimately. The latter could be a colleague, for example.

Now, think about them, each one at a time, and ask yourself the following questions, in this specific order:

1. Introversion (I) vs. Extraversion (E)

The Big Question: Are they introverts (I) or extraverts (E)?

- Follow-up Question: Where do you think they primarily get their energy from—after spending time alone or in quiet reflection (I), or around other people and engaging in social activities (E)?

2. Sensing (S) vs. Intuition (N)

The Big Question: How do they prefer to take in information?

- Follow-up Question: Do you think they are pragmatic, paying more attention to concrete facts, details, and present realities (S), or enjoy imagining abstract concepts and exploring theories (I)?

3. Thinking (T) vs. Feeling (F)

The Big Question: How do they make decisions?

- Follow-up Question: Do you think they tend to make decisions based on logic, objective analysis, and fairness (T), or prioritize personal values, harmony, and the impact on people's feelings (F)?

4. Judging (J) vs. Perceiving (P)

The Big Question: How do they prefer to organize their life and work?

- Follow-up Question: Do you think they like to have plans, schedules, and decisions settled in advance (J), or prefer to stay open to new information and keep their options flexible (P)?

By now, I am confident you must know where we are going. Based on your answers, keep the first letter that represents the most suitable answer (e.g., I for Introversion) for each of them.

You should end up with four letters, and you can now refer to the list of sixteen personalities to understand what their personality is likely to be and what it involves.

PUTTING IT INTO PRACTICE

Let's try a little role-play to see how well you identify these personalities. You're the new manager in the department, and you are sitting with your deputy, who's been there since the Ark, or maybe a bit earlier.

You: *We must review the supervisors to see which ones would best fit the couple of upcoming projects. Let's start with David.*

Deputy: Sure, I love this type of process, getting into and understanding what motivates people and how we can build a team together. I also think it's essential to base responsibilities on some basis rooted in ideals, so you're aiming high from the start. But why do you want to start with him?

You: *Well, he comes up first alphabetically, David Aardvark. What's he like?*

Deputy: *He's great, always there to help, often by my side in such moments, and won't say a bad thing about anybody in authority. I think he sometimes gets a bit agitated, like when his help isn't noticed or recognized.*

You: *I'd put him down as an ISFJ, with a wealth of empathy and loyalty. I suggest he leads the upcoming Office Management Projects, reorganizing the workflow structure. Ok, who's next?*

Deputy: *Well, there's dear Carole. It's pretty sweet how she loves structure and order. She has an excellent practical approach, but poor her, she hates it when things don't go to plan.*

You: *Most likely ISTJ, takes responsibility seriously, and has a love of order. She would be very well-suited to lead the implementation of the Compliance and Regulatory department. What about Gerry?*

Deputy: *Ah, Gerry, well, he couldn't be more different from Carole, like chalk and cheese. Gerry thrives when things don't go according to plan but is easily bored by routine. I believe he is an ESTP and that he will excel in conducting the next sales and marketing campaign. That only leaves Julia, and she's a real team player, always there for others, always seeing their point of view, always understanding. The only thing about her is that she gets upset when there's an unpleasantness or disagreement around the place. I can see how she feels because I don't like conflict too much either.*

You: *I'll put her down as ENFJ then, and she is likely to be a natural fit to lead the new Social Impact Programs in the Human Resource department. Let me see, I think that only leaves us with the research & development project to fill. Who do we have who fits that category? We're out of supervisors.*

Deputy: *Well, I really don't know. You need someone perceptive, forward-thinking, analytical, and has a wealth of empathy to manage the team.*

You: *Yes, I wonder who fits that role? Wait a moment... I know... You!*

Question: What is the personality type of your deputy that made you think he was the right fit for the research & development project?

Feel free to review the dialogue and the list of personality types again. The answer to the question is also included in the summary at the end of this section.

Any personality grouping can be perceived as an oversimplification, but when practiced correctly, the method provides valuable support for developing psychological intelligence and anticipating reactions.

When practiced, your analysis should be taken seriously and be deep enough to ensure accuracy. Do not make quick "judgments." For instance, you might see signs of anguish and think someone fits the ISFJ category (Defender), only to then notice the love of structure and routine and realize that the emotion you had thought to be anxiety is actually the stress of an ISTJ (Inspector).

The results of your analysis should never be definitive judgments on someone's personality, but recognition of more or less sensitivity to certain personality aspects.

The reality is that people will fit across categories, parts of one and parts of another, sometimes changing over time and evolving through self-awareness. Despite the generalization of this approach, it is a valuable exercise to start your mind filtering through and building up experience and knowledge in the field of psychological intelligence. As you get more experienced, you can intuitively choose how to act with different people and based on various situations.

Summary

- Myers and Briggs, daughter and mother respectively, developed the MBTI framework, which is highly recognized and widely used today, although it is not universally accepted within academic psychology.

- In recent years, websites have introduced user-friendly names for personality types to simplify the initial meaning of the MBTI framework.

- These are approaches that fit different personality types and that you can employ to read others.

- Understanding basic personality types is instrumental to emotional intelligence and applying the *Emotional Intelligence Theory*.

- Your deputy was an INFJ (Advocate). During the conversation, he said he "*love(s) this type of process, getting into and understanding what motivates people*," making him an insightful and empathetic leader—a quality he later confirms when referring to David by saying, "*Always there to help, often by my side in such moments.*" He is also stressed about how other feel when saying that he is like Julia, in this following statement: "*I can see how she feels because I don't like conflict too much either.*" Finally, the research & development project requires someone "*perceptive, forward-thinking, analytical, and has a wealth of empathy to manage the team,*" which seems to perfectly fit the *Advocate* profile being *Insightful*, *Empathetic*, and *Future-oriented*.

EMOTIONAL CUES: READING BETWEEN THE LINES

How you react emotionally to thousands of events daily determines who you are, and a significant part of emotional intelligence consists of recognizing these cues (psychological intelligence) and deciding how to react (which is related to *emotional agility*, the subject of the next chapter). This is when it's more about others than about yourself (unlike self-awareness and self-regulation).

Think of two politicians making speeches at the same rally. Politician A has no psychological intelligence, while Politician B has all he needs, with some left over, too.

Politician A struggles to read his audience. That means he cannot begin deciphering the signals they emit, and he continues as if nothing is amiss.

Politician B, on the other hand, can read his audience. She senses a growing anger at government policies, so she turns her attention to something she knows will be popular. The speech turns around midstream and swings decisively toward the far bank.

So, you're a politician dreaming of the big election, or a business leader trying to make things work within a budget so that you can generate profits. When you come up against people (not necessarily in a confrontational way, just interacting with them), you meet a range of emotions, which can be frustrating, bewildering, astonishing, surprising, or any other of the myriad emotions we encounter every day of the year.

Unless you are a hermit.

How do you recognize emotions? How do you interpret the signs so that you can respond positively?

Well, that's the heart of the matter about psychological intelligence. It is not about the language as we know it; it is more about silent language, expressed through attitudes, expressions, and postures, among others. There are six primary sources of signs to read and interpret emotions:

1. Microexpressions

Microexpressions, by definition, are brief and can be perceived as a reactive response to a change, often triggered by new information. They are intuitive and occur before the social filter kicks in, making them highly relevant to decoding emotions. These are predominantly expressed on people's faces, and you need to be very perceptive to capture them.

2. Body Language and Posture

Body language involves movements, usually to emphasize words or express emotions. At the same time, Posture is by definition more static and an unconscious statement of someone's stance on a specific topic or situation. Common examples include crossed arms, a form of being guarded, while open arms would signify receptivity.

3. Vocal Tone and Pace

Intonations and speed of speaking give away signs of hurry, calm, excitement, or nervousness, among so many others. Listening carefully to someone's message, as a whole, is critical (not just what is being said, but also how it is being said).

4. Clusters of Signals

A single cue, as sure as you may be of it, can be misleading. To be proven accurate, the cues should be recurring, or clustered, such as a combination of them carrying the same meaning. For example, crossed arms paired with a defensive tone are likely to mean that the person you are interacting with is not receptive to what you say.

5. Contextualize the Cues

Whatever is being expressed is situational: expressions, gestures, and words have different meanings depending on the situation, the culture, and personality involved in the interactions. It is part of the necessary empathy and understanding of the emotionally intelligent leader to consider all factors before concluding.

6. Empathetic Reflection

As previously stated, seeing situations from someone's perspective and feeling them from someone's heart—the core concept of empathy— are also necessary to understand others. When you think you do, use your empathy and allow the expression of self-vulnerability to confirm your understanding, such as asking, "It seems the current situation is getting to you and makes you feel sad, is my understanding correct?"

You have most likely already uncovered the characteristics you must develop to decode emotional cues: you must be receptive, observant, and actively listening. Qualities that an empathetic leader should possess.

The presence of mind in the moment is critical for developing an intuition for such reading and knowing how to respond.

The sooner you start, the sooner you will reach that level of natural competence.

CHAPTER SUMMARY: PSYCHOLOGICAL INTELLIGENCE

In this practical chapter covering psychological intelligence, we've examined broad classifications of personality types and, through a short role-play, illustrated how people might fit into these categories. Finally, we moved on to explore another aspect of psychological intelligence, one that is not based on personality types, but rather on how to read emotions.

Emotional cues are given off wherever we are. These are indications of how we feel at any given time. I tend to think of them as emotional clues, giving away our emotional state.

Applying this knowledge to practice, we learned ways to decipher emotional signs using specific abilities, which are being receptive, observant, and actively listening

And, of course, a little delve into what to come up with in response, because please bear in mind that this is a key part of emotional intelligence: not just recognizing the emotions of others (psychological intelligence) but developing the skills and experience to know how to respond to them (emotional agility).

PART 6
EMOTIONAL
AGILITY

FIFTH PRINCIPLE
BE AUTHENTIC

Being yourself is essential for interacting with others meaningfully, and authenticity can only be comfortably lived in the right environment. If it is lived in the right environment, it unavoidably leads to success.

CHAPTER

13

HOW TO ADAPT TO OTHERS

Emotional agility is about being aware of your thoughts and feelings, and being able to act in a way that is consistent with your values

— Dr. Susan David, psychologist at Harvard Medical School

DEFINITION

What better way to start this chapter than with a bestseller? Dr. Susan David's emotional agility topped the Wall Street Journal bestseller list in its category in 2016, establishing her as a leading voice in the field. She introduced and popularized the concept of *emotional agility*—a revolutionary approach to understanding and managing emotions that has since influenced psychology and leadership worldwide.

Rather than reiterate the full content here, let's have a look at the key concepts:

- Acknowledge and accept your emotions as they arise.

- Learn to step away from negative thoughts and emotional reactions.

- Be authentic and aligned with your values, even in emotional conflict.

- Approach social interactions with flexibility and courage.

Interestingly, *acknowledging and accepting your emotions as they arise* is closely related to self-awareness. Just as much as *learning to step away from negative thoughts and emotional reactions* is a form of self-regulation.

Being authentic and aligning with your values, even in emotional conflict, is a concept we will explore further in this chapter. For now, remember that yes, you can and must remain authentic, as there is no such thing as fake emotional intelligence.

Lastly, *approaching social interactions with flexibility and courage* is precisely what we will cover now. This statement is a perfect complement to psychological intelligence. Remember, as part of being emotionally intelligent is the capacity to read and understand others' emotions (psychological intelligence) and then tune in to the appropriate frequency to best deal with their emotions and reactions (emotional agility).

But why on earth is adapting to others important?

Well, think of how many people you meet on an average day. There are those with whom you have extensive relationships, such as your partner, children, parents, and work colleagues, all the way down to those you pass in the street, but it all amounts to a fair number of human beings.

Every one of those people will bring their own emotions into the field as they cross your field. To be fair, the passers-by may impart little emotion to your way, maybe a hint of frustration because you're blocking their path, or a look of wry amusement when someone walks right into you. Yet, the others, with whom you have significant contact, offer dozens more, and some of those will be in conflict. When we examined the personality types, we covered a wide range of traits and emotions, which will be expressed in different situations and at various levels of intensity.

This all amounts to a multitude of emotions; imagine them like lasers darting around in all directions. Some hit you straight on, while others glance off you. It doesn't stop the fact that they will keep coming.

Emotional agility enables us to navigate this complex web of moving parts, allowing us to respond appropriately.

It enables us to maximize the potential of every situation. Without abandoning authenticity, the emotionally agile person can respond with flexibility and empathy to the ever-changing emotions.

There is one other aspect here that, at first glance, might seem out of place, but please read on and have some faith.

It's the point about rigid reactions. You've probably all witnessed it at some point in your working lives. Whether born of fear of change or a lack of imagination, it comes to the same thing:

> *We have to go over the top into no man's land because*
> *that's how it's done.*

How many people went over the top because the generals were fully trained members of the rigid reaction brigade?

Look at it another way, which of these two words sounds more interesting, enticing, and fun?

> *Rigid*
>
> *Or*
>
> *Agile*

I don't think you need to answer that question to get the point. Rigid reactions are bad at the best of times, closing all options for you, but most importantly for others and the situation you're dealing with.

Summary

- Dr. Susan David invented the term emotional agility, which essentially includes self-awareness, self-regulation, authenticity, and flexibility.

- Psychological intelligence allows you to read and understand others. Emotional agility allows you to adapt and achieve the best outcome.

- The end game, the purpose behind all this nipping about, is to gain an advantage from every situation; that doesn't mean a selfish advantage. On the contrary, it's about benefiting everyone: the other person, you, and by extension, the situation.

BE YOURSELF

As we move on to emotional agility, we see that being emotionally intelligent also involves being consistent with what you hold dear, your values. And that they are a prerequisite to applying empathy within healthy parameters. As seen in the fifth *Emotional Intelligence Theory* principle, not only does authenticity help you *interact meaningfully with others*, but it also *leads to success*, provided that authenticity is *lived in the right environment*. Let's pause and think about it for a moment.

Imagine a tree, a very special tree, one that can choose its forest. As the tree moves from forest to forest, it is influenced by many environmental factors, including the other trees that provide shade around it, the sun, and the level of humidity, among many other factors.

Now, let's be more specific: This tree is a white oak.

The white oak will need sufficient space to grow, avoiding other trees that surround it from providing too much shade. It will also require enough rainfall and ample sunlight. Under such conditions, it is easy to imagine that its trunk will grow, its branches will flourish, and its roots will strengthen.

Now, imagine that same tree planted in a dense, shady forest—or among cactuses in an arid region. It is not difficult to imagine that this white oak, as special as it is, would not grow, flourish, or develop its roots; most likely, it may not even survive.

Well, humans are very much like this special white oak: They must remain authentic to who they are and choose a suitable environment to thrive. Through their choices, humans can move and establish themselves in suitable environments or be misled in their choices and never reach their full potential.

For their environment to be deemed healthy, they must benefit from sufficient happiness and learning, just as the sun and rain benefit our white oak. They must also have enough space, enough freedom, without too much shade or control, to avoid being overshadowed. And, if and only if these conditions are aligned, humans, much like white oaks, will develop, grow, and flourish.

But how does it relate to emotional agility?

Another way of putting it is that being authentic means being honest with ourselves and others, which is essential for responding to situations in a way that stays true to our values, while also acknowledging and adapting to the emotions of others. In other words, it's a genuine reaction, yet with an element of control, because we're empathetic humans.

To interact meaningfully with others, we utilize empathy from our authentic perspective, which involves compassion and kindness within a defined framework guided by our values. Emotional agility, however, is governed by the ability to understand and adapt to others' emotions, to use empathy best, and connect. Both are essential to becoming emotionally intelligent.

Let's unravel that series of statements on empathy and emotional agility.

Leaving our good old white oak behind, think of a path on a mountain called Mount Understanding, branching off into smaller paths, some leading to the peak, and some others leading nowhere. You start walking from the valley, and reaching its peak, high up on the mountain, is your objective. In other words, understanding others.

However, along the way, you will need to make choices, such as following a different route or cutting across the forest that dresses up the mountain. There are several ways from the valley floor to the top of the mountain.

The choices you make along the way matter just as much as the emotions you choose when interacting with others, and you may even alter or influence the mountain landscape to navigate your way to the top more easily, just as you would use empathy to influence others and their emotions.

It is still you climbing the mountain, being authentic to your rhythm and route preferences, following the different paths of understanding, until you reach the mountain top where the person you are interacting with is waiting for you, with trust, respect, and ultimately loyalty.

That's an inroad into understanding emotional agility and, through it, understanding others.

The word agility precisely suggests the ability to change quickly, to jump from one path to another. It suggests fitness, sureness, and fleetness of foot. These 'ness' words are nouns that speak of good responses, including the capability of changing direction mid-course. We admire people who are fleet of foot, using adjectives such as flexible and adaptable.

Being emotionally agile means being confident in yourself and true to who you are, while also adapting enough to meet others and earn their trust, respect, and loyalty.

CHAPTER SUMMARY: EMOTIONAL AGILITY

We began by examining emotional agility, reasoning that it is the ability to adapt with both authenticity and flexibility to interact effectively with others and manage their emotions.

As we delved into this key concept of emotional intelligence, we realized that we need it every day because every encounter with another person involves an exchange of emotions, however slight.

We choose agility over rigidity because rigidity is often spurred by either fear or a lack of imagination. It enables us to adapt to emotions, which is the final step before using emotional intelligence and empathy to engage with others.

To prove it, we climbed Mount Understanding, navigating our way through different routes of understanding, staying true ourselves, to finally reach the peak, where the person we were interacting with was waiting for us, to lend us trust, respect, and show that if we can stay atop that mountain, we could even benefit from loyalty.

CHAPTER

14

CONFLICT RESOLUTIONS

> *"Peace is not the absence of conflict; it is the ability to handle conflict by peaceful means."*
> — *Ronald Reagan, 40th U.S. President*

LEVERAGING EMOTIONAL AGILITY

"I'm sorry, and I know you've just got home after an all-nighter, but Jake has lost it with the test failures, and he says he's quitting and not coming back. You know, sometimes even I wonder what we're trying to do here."

I was exhausted. No, I'd left exhaustion behind some time ago, entering into some ghostly realm where severe-looking electronic test engineers specialized in shaking their heads and repeating no, nyet, nein, and non.

"Ed, don't bail on me now. You're a major part of the company. Listen, tell Jake to meet me at the café on the corner of 24th and Main. I'll be there in... twenty minutes. I'll square it away with him first, then we can have a good chat."

"He won't talk to me, so I'll send him a text. He's bent over his phone in the car park, so he'll get it."

I had two things on my side. First, I had twenty minutes to work out a plan. Second, Jake hadn't left the car park at work; that meant he didn't really mean to leave his employment.

I settled on the grim pancake plan. That involves sharing his frustration (a perfectly genuine emotion because nobody wanted to get these products through testing more than I, the owner), plus a strong dose of sugar (either maple syrup or blueberry jam) and some warming caffeine. My plan involved a lot of empathy, recognizing that not only had Jake put every waking moment into these products for the last two months, but also his reputation was on the line.

He felt a mix of frustration and hurt pride. That's a challenging but common combination, particularly keenly felt by those who value recognition. Apart from eating pancakes, my plan involved including him in the solution. It meant a lot of listening as he vented; then, as he calmed down, we moved on to the next steps, and he put aside his pride and frustration, becoming enthusiastic once more.

With Ed, it was a different matter. As the financial controller, he was dedicated, precise, and to the point, with everything fitting the mold or not.

He didn't think Jake fitted any mold he had ever seen.

What I did with Ed was six circuits of the wrap-around car park that surrounded the office. I laid out the facts.

"We need Jake, Ed. Nobody has the technical experience of our products as much as him."

"He's not a team player, never has been, never will."

"And"—this was my clincher, because Geoff, the general manager, was coming up for retirement—"that's precisely why he will never be GM."

"Who will be?" Ah, that was interesting. I had always seen Ed in a support role as the perfect number two. Did he have the ambition to move up?

"That's between you and the sales director..." I was thinking on my feet, my senses alert to how this vital person would react.

"Well, not me for sure. I'm happy as I am."

"That's that, then, but we won't do it yet. I want to get through this test first, and I don't think Al's quite ready yet. I want to give him some interim assignments outside of sales to see how he does. I think he's too pushy and disinclined to see the other side at the moment."

That was an unplanned morning's work. I'd dealt with two very different but typical personalities. Jake, gung-ho but not a team player, had been folded back into the team by teasing the solution out of him. With Steady Eddie, it had been a case of sharing strategic decisions with him, plus giving him a strong dose of reassurance. As I drove home, I considered two things:

1. These were two very typical personality types, both exhibiting the kind of emotions one would expect.

2. I had to admit it, I'd done alright in sorting out two people who were vital to the organization. Most of this was because, despite my exhaustion, I could see where my empathy had led me.

3. Actually, I tell a lie, for a third reflection went through my mind, how Ed and I had seen Jake's response so differently. We both interpreted the situation in entirely different ways. Ed had never gotten on with Jake and wanted to build the company without

his involvement. I'd used my psychological intelligence to read the situation and work out a solution. I'd seen what Ed hadn't been able to see and used that to work out a solution.

Not a bad morning's work after all.

BALANCING RATIONAL THINKING
AND EMOTIONAL SENSITIVITY

This subheading has a grand-sounding element to it, using words that psychologists will trip out on daily but don't mean an awful lot to the rest of us.

But the reality is both straightforward and incredibly sweet. That's not sweet like candy, but sweet like everything coming together.

There's a reason for this. Let's experiment to illustrate that reason. List the worst, most nerve-racking problems you've had to deal with. Don't stop listing until you've exhausted yourself. We aim to address some challenging and thought-provoking issues.

Now, think about the solutions you employed. The employee walking out with the drawings for your new design was resolved with a bit of diplomacy because you knew Engineer A had been passed over for promotion. He loves your business and felt he was forced to leave. Meanwhile, when Scientist B dropped dead one Monday morning, taking with him all the latest discoveries, you created a team called The Recovery Team and successfully delved into all their minds to recreate what you thought you had lost. In particular, you have people working together to come up with the goods collectively.

When Salesman C came in, running his fingers through his thinning hair, crying out that he had just messed up and lost your biggest customer, you got on the phone and spent an hour of valuable time telling jokes with the chairperson of the customer. The last joke was about an Englishman, an Irishman, and... well, you won the customer back again.

What makes it all so wonderfully simple is that there is a common thread running through here.

It's called empathy.

It arises because you've taken the time to get to know yourself, finding ways to understand what motivates others. You read them and understand them. You adapted to their emotions, using a suitable set of emotions. You build on this by applying emotional intelligence.

Another way of looking at it is that *every cloud has a silver lining*. Or *it's an ill wind that blows no good*. Every situation, however dire it may seem, has something positive somewhere within it. By understanding people's emotions and reactions, by feeling with them, you can harness this good through emotional intelligence.

Then, you can use it in an open and cooperative way, carrying people with you. It's more than saying *more hands make light work* because it has the element of inspiration in it, of genuine, authentic leading by example.

Hence, you're not just carrying people along, you're exciting and empowering them. This can't happen in a vacuum; you must live and breathe empathy to get there.

Remember, first, get to know yourself; this is the beginning of everything. Then, learn to regulate your natural tendencies. This is important so you don't give unhelpful automatic reactions. Instead, use your psychological intelligence to read and understand others, adapt, and work out the best way forward emotionally.

Third (and last, I promise), by adapting emotionally, you can apply empathy from this point on to solve the situation at hand.

CHAPTER SUMMARY: CONFLICT RESOLUTION

At the beginning of this chapter, we efficiently resolved a conflict, handling two distinct personalities with different objectives and purposes, utilizing both our psychological intelligence to read and understand them and our emotional agility to manage the emotions at play, thereby resolving the conflict to the best of our ability.

Through this story, we proved that these concepts, coupled with empathy, help reduce conflicts.

Once we can read and understand others, we can adapt appropriately; it's then a remarkably straightforward process to use empathy from there.

Yes, it takes investment and the use of those grey cells, but the benefits far outweigh the cost.

PART 7
EMOTIONAL INTELLIGENCE
BEYOND THE WORKPLACE

CHAPTER

15

EMOTIONAL INTELLIGENCE IN YOUR PERSONAL LIFE

"When you show deep empathy toward others, their defensive energy goes down, and positive energy replaces it. That's when you can get more creative in solving problems."
— *Stephen R. Covey, U.S. author, educator, and businessman*

BEYOND WORK: A MORE FULFILLING LIFE

"I know exactly why he's unhappy."

"Why, then, Supermind?"

"Because he's selfish and doesn't seem to be able to manage or conquer it."

That set me thinking. The gentleman in question was racing ahead in his career and had a busy social life to boot. By traditional reckoning, he should be 'as happy as Larry.'

The fact that this person is called Larry should not cause too much confusion.

My friend with the super mind explained a bit more. She explained that true happiness depends on being emotionally intelligent and having empathy.

"Larry just can't do that. He knows himself well enough. I mean, I've experienced him on retreats where we practice meditation to connect with our inner selves. He excels at this, just like he's streaking ahead at work. Didn't he used to work for you, and now you report to him?"

"Yeah, but I agree he's not a happy guy."

"That's because he's only got one side of the equation. You see, he lacks empathy. Remember what empathy is?"

"Yeah," I replied, being a 'yeah' type of guy. "It's when you can put yourself in someone else's shoes, seeing the world as they see it."

"Exactly. Larry just cannot grasp that concept."

"Yeah, but"—another of my favorite sentence-openers—"he often seems happy. I mean, beautiful girl on his arm, fab car, vacations in the Caribbean, and so on."

"Yeah, but," Supermind replied, making gentle fun of my stock answers, "when did he last have a long-term relationship?"

"Never," I replied.

That was the point. Larry got on at work because there wasn't much emotional intelligence in play in those days—although that was changing with people like me working their way steadily up the corporation—but translated it to his social life, and he was miserable personified.

Although he had a flashy appearance, he superficially seemed as if everything was going his way.

Larry had done half the equation but lacked the other half. Another way of looking at it is that he had mastered self-awareness and done quite a good job with self-regulation, but he got a resounding 'F' when it came to being caring and emotionally intelligent with others. He couldn't grasp that others had thoughts, ideas, attitudes, and emotions. It was almost as if he were the only one alive in a sea of cardboard cutouts.

Larry got married three times and divorced three times, too. He rose to the top at work but was then ousted in a boardroom reshuffle that saw a new chairperson who believed in emotional intelligence.

I could invent a poignant ending for the *Life of Larry*, but the truth is I lost touch with him. The last I heard, for many years, he was an ageing ski instructor living in a chalet and drinking too much.

Then I bumped into Supermind again. She had an update on Larry, and it has a happy ending. He got off the excess of alcohol and finally, broke and with no job, found this thing called empathy.

He now works in a modest job in another town where he and his (fourth) wife are very happy as they bring up their three kids. She had been instrumental in helping him develop emotional intelligence.

"Yeah," I said. "So he finally got the link between empathy and personal fulfillment in life?"

"Yeah," Supermind replied. "He's now a paid-up member of the *Emotional Intelligence Theory*."

STRENGTHENING BONDS
WITH EMOTIONAL INTELLIGENCE

Let's stick with the personal front for a moment longer. Larry's case is a typical one, so much so that we can almost make Larry's Law out of it:

> *Larry says emotional intelligence is vital in building bilateral relationships, whether romantic, family, or friends.*
>
> *Larry says, 'Believe me, I tried to go without it, and it didn't work.'*

And here's where it gets interesting because—like it or not—there's a definite link between work and personal life here. As people no longer need to travel to work, since work comes to them, settling in their homes, the connection between the workplace and home has never been as thin as it is today.

Not only that, but more time spent at home also led people to spend more time with each other, fostering a new intensity in relationships that requires care, understanding, and adaptability—traits that emotional intelligence broadly encompasses.

That doesn't mean it was never there, but there is recognition that what works in the working world also works at home.

That's why Larry, three decades into adulthood, became emotionally intelligent at his new job, but only after seeing it in his personal life with his new wife. She taught him the benefits of truly understanding people, essentially by putting on their shoes and walking with them.

Let's try an experiment to make the point. Pick an example of a work problem. No, don't tell me, at least not yet. Now, pick a personal issue—

this could be with your spouse, a friend, or a family member, as long as it is relationship-based.

Now, do some analysis of both problems. The aim is to work out what went wrong in each case.

The root is likely going to be the same in each case.

Whether it's a lack of trust, respect, communication, or a dozen different possibilities, the chances are strong that where you have a problem in one sphere of your life, you will find 'similar but different' problems in the other.

This is because it all comes down to relationships and how you nurture them. It's how you communicate and interact with your wife, with your colleagues, and also with your boss. It's how you deal with your neighbors, just as you deal with the sales department or production.

Relationships hinge on the need to interact with the other party in a fair, open, and consistent manner, taking into account their needs, wants, fears, and emotions.

It comes down to being emotionally intelligent.

CHAPTER SUMMARY: LIVING A HAPPY LIFE

It's always fun to apply practices from one part of life to another. And that is what we are talking about. We're discussing the fact that emotional intelligence knows no boundaries. As the set of skills develops, its benefits expand into one's personal life, supporting situations that are sometimes even more complex and demanding than those in the workplace.

We first examined the importance of empathy in personal life. This is because the ability to see things from others' perspectives is a foundation of true happiness. Likewise, with the capability to be fair, kind, and communicative, it benefits our personal relationships.

In doing so, we've also gone full circle. We began our journey by laying the foundation of the *Emotional Intelligence Theory*, which is encapsulated by five key principles. We then understood that the spearhead of those principles was emotional intelligence; thus, we had to become self-aware and gain insight into ourselves. Now, having become so, and by self-regulating and employing empathy to walk in the shoes of others, we've come back to the beginning, examining how this helps us lead happy lives in which giving and receiving are merged into one.

A world of understanding, well worth living.

CONCLUSION

Remember back when we first heard about the department store's floor manager coming to terms with the 80:20 rule? By applying the *Emotional Intelligence Theory*, the same department store manager can now focus efficiently on the 20% that yields 80% of the intended results: People.

Challenges create opportunities, and as attracting and retaining talent has settled as the key challenge in most industries, as a leader in business, you need to know how to capitalize on this situation.

The big question is how, and the *Emotional Intelligence Theory* set out to do precisely that—laying out the foundations, built on understanding and adaptability, to uncover your emotional intelligence, applied and practiced through its theory.

It may sound like a lot to absorb, but most of the concepts described in this book will soon become second nature and common sense.

Emotional intelligence consists of five blocks: self-awareness, self-regulation, and empathy, which form the foundation of your emotional intelligence; and then psychological intelligence and emotional agility, which enable you to adapt to others.

Aristotle said, *"Knowing yourself is the beginning of all wisdom."* The very reason why self-awareness is a steppingstone is that understanding yourself leads to understanding others, and in turn, to your capacity to connect meaningfully, which is, in itself, the essence of emotional intelligence.

The book describes typical personality types, but with the provision that these are indications only and should be taken for what they are— broad categories that will lead you in the right direction but as guides, not gospel. Thus, the book also gives some broad categories of ways to detect emotional cues, including microexpressions, body language and posture, vocal tone and pace, clusters of signals, context, and empathetic reflection. These big buckets lead to deciphering situations, allowing you to remain agile and anticipate.

The emotionally intelligent person wants to know about these categories because awareness of them is a tool they can use to navigate social contexts effectively.

But it doesn't just come down to a quick personality test and Bob's your uncle, everything is sorted out. And because practice does not make perfection, but self-awareness initiates it, there are practical ways to get to know yourself, including self-reflection, feedback, emotional audits, and mindfulness. Feedback is an interesting one because it's often perceived as a negative for several reasons, including the fear of facing self-vulnerability, whereas it's, in fact, a precious gift. Sharing feedback is equally important and contributes to the virtuous circle, encapsulated by one of the principles of the *Emotional Intelligence Theory*. Genuine, effective feedback follows a formula that involves honesty, regularity, and fairness. The outputs are far more concrete because we're establishing action plans, corrective encouragement, and further feedback at a later date.

John Hancock said that the most outstanding ability in business is to get along with others and influence their actions. That's powerful, but then John Hancock had a sound emotional dashboard. This is similar to the dials on your car dashboard; it tells you how you're doing. Knowing how you react to certain situations is vital to avoid overreactions, automatic responses, and negative tendencies, which your emotional dashboard can help you with.

And when things go wrong, as they inevitably will, we examine how to reset under pressure, using self-regulation to manage situations. Likewise, we discussed the importance of taking a breath, then reframing and channeling energies to solve problems, whether inherited from others or caused by ourselves. This often involves calming yourself down, so you can then calm others. This is all about staying in control, or regaining it, rather than panicking when and if you lose it.

Psychological intelligence, defined as the *ability to understand how people react and behave in particular circumstances*, is a crucial part of the *Emotional Intelligence Theory*. This, along with empathy and emotional intelligence, enables us to broaden our perspective to include others, having already achieved a level of self-awareness and self-regulation, and being ready to adapt to them. We're dealing now with the interaction between you and other people.

It's now time to put this into practice with empathy leading the way. Remember, empathy is about putting yourself in someone else's shoes and walking a mile in their shoes.

Also, remember that we're bound to encounter some empathy deniers; that's just part of the course. They will say empathy is weakness, causing endless indecisiveness and no clear path to follow. The answer to that is that empathy requires extraordinary courage and strength. It's the recognition that you need to be open-minded first and decisive second, that makes the difference; otherwise, you're charging in there without any idea what the options are.

That's hardly the best way to go about it.

Emotional agility is the next aspect we examined, which is a marriage between awareness of your feelings and consistency with your values (remember the Venn diagram where the shared area between universal, personal, and corporate values creates a safe and secure operating location for the use of empathy). At this stage, it's about choices on the journey up to

Mount Understanding, where others are waiting for you at the peak to lend you their precious respect and trust, which you must cherish and protect.

We're now very close to resolving the mystery of impactful leadership. This is where we can utilize emotional agility, along with the other skills we've acquired, to resolve issues and bring people along with us.

Because, at the end of the day, this is all about people and taking them with you to create a better environment, which carries positive ripple effects spreading across. As we develop our emotional intelligence, we learn that what we give comes back to us, often many times over. You end up with behavioral skills you've developed, namely emotional intelligence, which add to what you offer the world of work. This brings us neatly back to the Gen Z and Millennial generations, which you may also be part of, and what they bring to the table in terms of flexibility and original thinking. By operating flexibly and thoughtfully, you naturally develop an appeal for what you represent, using emotional intelligence as your competitive advantage.

Finally, this book takes us back to the self, completing a circle. We started our journey looking at ourselves. Then, we broadened our scope and explored the fascinating areas surrounding us, led by example and empathy. Now, we can examine how to apply this to our personal lives, focusing on building relationships based on trust and respect and developing solutions to problems at home, just as we have learned to do at work.

That is emotional intelligence, built in, deep within you, making its principles rule your decisions. It's the values that guide our emotional intelligence, enabling us to lead with confidence, knowing that we're bringing others along with us. They share the journey with us because they want to. They passionately connect with your purpose because they want to.

The world, whether at work or play, becomes all the stronger for that inclusion.

ORIGAMI EDITIONS
READING FOR BETTER LIVING

BETTER YOU SERIES

Printed in Great Britain
by Amazon